UNIVERSITY LIBR
W. S. U. ▪ STEVENS

D0866562

ADOLESCENTS IN SCHOOL

by Claude E. Buxton

New Haven and London
Yale University Press
1973

Copyright ©1973 by Yale University.
All rights reserved. This book may not be
reproduced, in whole or in part, in any form
(except by reviewers for the public press),
without written permission from the publishers.
Library of Congress catalog card number: 72-91290
International standard book number: 0-300-01617-4

Designed by Sally Sullivan
and set in IBM Century type.
Printed in the United States of America by
The Murray Printing Co., Forge Village, Mass.

Published in Great Britain, Europe, and Africa by
Yale University Press, Ltd., London.
Distributed in Canada by McGill-Queen's University
Press, Montreal; in Latin America by Kaiman & Polon,
Inc., New York City; in Australasia and Southeast
Asia by John Wiley & Sons Australasia Pty. Ltd.,
Sydney; in India by UBS Publishers' Distributors Pvt.,
Ltd., Delhi; in Japan by John Weatherhill, Inc., Tokyo.

CONTENTS

LA
217
.B89

Acknowledgments   ix

Part 1: Growing and Schooling   1

1. Exploring Adolescence   3
2. Studying Adolescents in School   7
3. Adolescents in School   12
4. Changing for the Better and Problems to Be Expected   19

Part 2: Empirical Studies   31

5. Choosing a Method   33
6. The Chosen Method and the Schools in Which It Was
   Used   41
7. Intensity and Direction of Attitudes toward School   57
8. Patterns of Adolescent Attitudes toward School   87
9. Another Component of Attitude and a Replication   98
10. Summary and Comment   118

Appendixes   125
Bibliography   175
Index   177

223739

Figures

1. Mean Degree of Positive and Active Liking,
   Schools A, B, and C   59
2. Mean Degree of Generalized Dislike,
   Schools A, B, and C   63
3. Mean Degree of Conscientiousness, Schools A, B, and C   66
4. Mean Degree of Anxiety-Guilt, Schools A, B, and C   69
5. Mean Degree of Liking for Teachers, Schools A, B,
   and C   73
6. Mean Degree of Social Distractibility, Schools A,
   B, and C   77
7. Mean Degree of Orientation toward Future,
   Schools A, B, and C   80
8. Mean Degree of Positive and Active Liking, School D   105
9. Mean Degree of Generalized Dislike, School D   107
10. Mean Degree of Conscientiousness, School D   108
11. Mean Degree of Anxiety-Guilt, School D   108
12. Mean Degree of Liking for Teachers, School D   109
13. Mean Degree of Social Distractibility, School D   110
14. Mean Degree of Orientation toward Future, School D   110
15. Mean Degree of Liking for School as a Social
    System, School D   111

Tables

1. Reliability Coefficients for Specific Scales and Schools   49
2. Intercorrelations of the Seven Scales in Schools A,
   B, and C, Boys Only   90
3. Intercorrelations of the Seven Scales in Schools A,
   B, and C, Girls Only   95
4. Intercorrelations of the Eight Scales Used in School D   115

ACKNOWLEDGMENTS

My greatest debt is to the students, teachers, and administrators who cooperated with me in this study. Many teachers and administrators clearly went out of their way to aid me in finding out what their students felt about statements I asked them to rate, without making requests for an immediate "payoff" from the study or from me. It is my strong hope that the results and interpretive remarks presented here will enable those responsible for our school systems to join in the tremendously difficult and essential task of modifying our schools. That they will need help from students and the community alike seems inevitable to me.

I could not have carried on this work without the generous and extremely patient support of the Charles F. Kettering Foundation. Despite my reporting essentially no progress in my early annual reports, I was given quite cheerful backing, to the point where one official of the foundation remarked he was glad to learn that sometimes other people also "couldn't make a dime."

It gives me much pleasure that I can write this book not only as a professor of psychology at Yale University, but also as a Fellow of its recently established Center for Studies of Education.

Various secretaries in the Department of Psychology offices shared in typing preliminary drafts and pieces of drafts. The final typing was done by Mrs. Marilyn Stiles. Computer assistance was given by Mr. and Mrs. John Dow.

PART 1:
GROWING AND SCHOOLING

It is not easy to know the mind of an adolescent. In recent years, however, a number of explorations have been made by psychoanalysts, psychologists, sociologists, and others. Each scholar makes a particular contribution in his way, but we cannot with confidence claim that this very large and very important group of people whom we call adolescents is thoroughly understood. And it is important that they should be, for they are on their way to parenthood, governance, the life of work and leisure, and everything else that makes up adulthood (which does not constitute a claim that everyone reaches a full-fledged adulthood).

We can understand why it is not easy to know the mind of an adolescent if we stop to think of what we now believe him to be. (I say "him" only for simplicity of expression.) For one thing, an adolescent is in a period of development in which he characteristically is seeking autonomy and selfhood (see the empathic book by Erik Erikson, *Identity: Youth and Crisis*, 1968). The idea that other people claiming to be students of adolescence should invade his privacy, know his innermost feelings about himself and about his relations to others or the world about him, is likely to be repugnant to him unless he has great confidence and trust in the person who would understand him.

As part of this growth toward identity and selfhood, the adolescent is involved in formulating attitudes toward what he does or what people expect him to do. Often those attitudes are not exactly clear, or they vacillate. Something blurted in anger one day may not be true the next. But, ordinarily, as a young person proceeds through adolescence there is increasing stability of attitudes, of self-expectations, of relationships with others, and so on, until adulthood can be said to be reached.

In addition to striving for a sense of self, the adolescent is subject to other pressures or strivings which arise as a result of the physiological changes occurring in him (see chap. 1 of *Normal Adolescence*, by the Group for the Advancement of Psychiatry, 1968). He has for years been learning a sex role, more or less clearly defined for him by his culture, and as he moves into puberty, sexuality becomes an ever more significant aspect of all

3

phases of growth and development. New sensitivities and a new
awareness of society's expectations can be disturbing, whether
he accepts such expectations as proper or rebels against them as
out-of-date or otherwise inappropriate. Part of the difficulty here
lies in the fact that sex education, especially of a kind concerned
with the relations among people, and their significance, tends to
be a taboo subject, even causing political division or worse in
some communities (see Cottle 1971, pt. 2, for a drastic example).
Thus the schools are not allowed to deal with a subject they
might more competently handle than does word-of-mouth communication (presumably often incompetent or misleading) and
the other procedures which adolescents can hardly be stopped
from using in learning about this aspect of their developing hu-
manity. It further should be said that while some of the objec-
tions to introducing this kind of concern into the schools are
seemingly based on either religious grounds or the argument that
parents have the right to determine what their offspring learn, it
is quite likely that part of the resistance is due to fear and anxiety rearoused in adults (parents, teachers, administrators) as a
conscious or unconscious remnant of their own adolescence.

Since early childhood, the adolescent has been sorting out the
world of people. The process presumably begins as a recognition
of *I-everyone else* and progresses to a *we-they* feeling which
tends to become stronger during adolescence. *We*, in this case, is
an adolescent and a set of cohorts at about the same stage of development. *They*, of course, are mainly the adults in one's life.
They get subdivided into parents, teachers, and other categories,
and the *we*s may respond quite differently to the various adult
groups (think of the responses of sixteen-year-old boys to their
athletic coaches and to their fathers). The *we* part of this classification is the often-discussed peer group (again, see *Normal
Adolescence*, pp. 68-70). This group may be very significant in
the development of any particular adolescent, for its members
are in one way or another going through about the same experience. They provide understanding and tutoring; they share one's
concerns about life, self, and society; and they support rehearsal
of behaviors deemed important in becoming adult, or reactions
against what is seen as adult dampening of youthful expressions
of feeling or individuality.

It is also clear in recent decades, and must have been for a long
time, that adolescence is a time of continual exploring, question-

ing, doubting, testing. This may be more true of certain social-class or ethnic or geographical groups than others, but the latter general problem has received scant attention. Yet it is hard to believe that anyone can pass directly from childhood to adulthood without experiencing these reactions to at least some degree. There are indications that adolescence is beginning at an earlier chronological age (Tanner 1962, p. 143) and that it is being forced by society to last longer. For example, Keniston (in Erikson 1963, pp. 191-220) suggests that in our increasingly technological times, adolescents cannot as often as they would like secure jobs that signify independence, readiness for marriage, and so on unless they are willing to extend their period of dependence by continuing schooling or training. Cottle (1971, p. 180) refers to the impression in suburban high schools of "suspending adolescents between what should have been the goals of childhood and what clearly can wait for adulthood." And Goodman (1962, pp. 134-35) harks back to the theme of the short supply of meaningful jobs for the young. Presumably such things are known at least dimly to adolescents, even though they may not yet have reached the level of development at which they feel ready for a job and independence, and the facts of life are painfully conspicuous to many of those who are in college, or even in high school, without wishing to be there. Again, there must be variations in this length-of-adolescence theme across social-class, ethnic, or other lines, but most of what we think we know focuses on the white middle-class American adolescent.

It has been noted in recent years that, along with everything else that is changing at a rapid pace, the quality of adolescence is changing also. By the term *quality*, I mean the kinds of things that happen as part of adolescence, the problems that must be solved, the tasks that must be accomplished. For example, Friedenberg (1959, p. 203) summarizes his analysis of what is happening to adolescence by saying that it is disappearing, i.e., society is changing in such a way that it makes finding one's identity—a central task in adolescence—more and more difficult. A parallel idea is advanced by Keniston and was stated in the preceding paragraph. Quite apart from such opinions, it would seem that what we perceive as unsatisfactory in our society—unwanted war, poverty, racism, sex discrimination, pollution, failure to conserve what should be conserved, urban problems, problems of the elderly, resources inadequate to match a burgeoning population—cannot but have an impact on the adolescent who is trying to work out his value system, his life direction and style, and so many other personal matters which depend in large part on interactions with his society—its expectations of him and his expectations of it.

Since adolescents do not ordinarily discuss, at least with behavioral scientists, private feelings about matters such as those which appear to be confidently described in the last few pages, can we really believe what is reported? I think the answer is that we can treat such statements as fairly legitimate inferences from what adolescents do or say, or what we may learn from the occasional (how representative?) adolescent who trusts and talks to us. At best we have to retain a margin of doubt, because we know from personal experiences and what other adults tell us that even self-perception and knowledge are capable of distortion, that influence by unrealized forces of self-defense may be at work, or the expectations of other people or their attitudes concerning one's self may unwittingly cause us (including adolescents) to try to live up to (or down to) a self-image we get partly from others.

Finally, it seems necessary to remark that not only at the college level, which has had more of the headlines, but at the school level the students (in this case, adolescents) are changing. Although it may be regarded as a separate problem by some, it does not seem possible to separate the influences of the changing nature of adolescents from the pressures for change they and others exert on teachers, administrators, and schools. Many times in the recent past, failure to adapt by those in charge of the schools has resulted in confrontation, dissatisfaction, or outright rebellion on the part of students and even teachers. This is not likely to change until adult (including parental) resistance to change can be modified through an understanding of adolescence and a willingness to admit that adult defensiveness is in part a resonance to one's own adolescence, though largely forgotten so far as consciousness is concerned, but still having an influence by way of the kind of person it made one into as an adult. Once openness and willingness to understand adolescence are achieved, it becomes desirable, even essential, to update that understanding as adolescents become somewhat different when each new age group comes along.

2. STUDYING ADOLESCENTS IN SCHOOL

Having said all that we have about the problems and pressures of growing up, we have now to remind ourselves that a goodly part of the adolescent's life is spent in school, a place where there are authority figures, peers, and tasks which may be enjoyed or disliked; where certain kinds of development (such as ability to handle language or numbers or technical instruments or tools, not to mention social skills and moral standards) are expected; and where there are many rules as well as, in many cases, parental expectations so clear that they might well be written on the walls.

Criticizing schools and pointing out their imagined and real failures has been something of an indoor sport among free-lance writers, teachers, college professors, and many others for the last decade or more (and perennially before that, we may safely assume). Our concern presently is not with that important matter, but it may be relevant to mention that one of the most recent and evenhanded, well-documented treatments of it is Charles Silberman's *Crisis in the Classroom*, 1970. Part 2 and sections of part 4 are especially helpful as background for the problems we shall discuss later. One of Silberman's concerns is, of course, for educational reform, and he discusses reforms that have been advocated or tried in the past; usually the results have been the kind that make Sarason (1971) remark in several places on the truth of the old saying "The more things change, the more they remain the same." The problem of school organization or structure is one that we shall discuss specifically in chapter 4 because it does indeed pertain to how adolescents react to school.

Most studies of adolescence are concerned with the developmental process in general, and schooling enters the picture only as one aspect of the many experiences which are part of the process of maturing. Certain sociologists have had more direct interest in the adolescent in school and have studied him there, in some instances making primary use of questionnaires, supplemented by informal interviews (Coleman 1961), and in other cases balancing the use of questionnaires by other "objective" procedures as well as interviews—e.g., the important studies of Friedenberg (1959) and his associates, and also Nordstrom et al. (1967) and Friedenberg (1963). Keniston (e.g., *Young Radicals*, 1968) has used not only interviews but psychological tests and other procedures. All these studies shed light on the value systems, the status systems, and personality development of adolescents as seen by researchers working within the school setting. Yet, as with any developmental process, there always remain questions which there was not time or opportunity to study. And new questions arise. For example, it seems to have been taken for granted not merely that every child should go to school, but, in many segments of our population, that the more schooling he gets, the better off he is likely to be. This assumption is currently being challenged as a reflection of the additional, almost unquestioned, assumption that the purpose of schooling is to prepare students for later life (as though, somehow, they were not already living *in* school). It is hoped, then, that it will be helpful in our understanding of adolescence if we attempt to inquire further into the reactions of adolescents to school, for there is no doubt of widespread concern among them about the meaning of school for what they are to do and be in the world, as well as of their sensitivity to those assumptions just mentioned.

What Do We Want to Learn?

Everything written above suggests that, taking the school as it exists, we may well ask: how do the students feel about it? Perhaps the first thing to note is that this seemingly straightforward question in fact points to a chicken/egg problem. That is, the way adolescents feel about school is surely shaped in part by what the school does to them (in the jargon, one "output" produced by the school is the student's feelings about it). But at the same moment we realize that what the student does in school, or how well he does it, depends upon how he feels about it (so feelings are also an "input," so far as schooling is concerned). In studying how adolescents feel about school, then, we are doing two things simultaneously. One is an attempt to add to our knowledge about school, in the sense of learning what it seems to produce as reactions in adolescents. The other is an attempt to add to our knowledge about adolescence, in the sense of learning how or to what extent any student's feelings can reflect his living part of his life in school. The first kind of knowledge might lead us to wish to change the school in the interests of producing certain more favorable reactions. The second may enhance our understanding of adolescence itself, as revealed through the contribution of schooling to the young person's feelings.

To sharpen our language somewhat, let us substitute the word *attitude* for the word *feeling*, defining an attitude as a predisposition to react in a certain way if a certain event or situation occurs. Thus we can speak of attitudes toward school, knowing there are predispositions to react in certain ways toward many different aspects of school, or many different events in school, and they are coexistent in the individual students. We do not know just how many attitudes we could discover, but we can be sure some of them would be very difficult to detect or subtle to measure, so we shall limit our study to a relatively small number of obviously pertinent and widely discoverable attitudes.

We know further, at least in general, that attitudes are likely to change somewhat as students proceed through the school. One of the less commonly studied age periods is that of adolescence. So we shall, as one of our goals, try to discover variations in the attitudes among students in grades 7 to 12 inclusive, which in the schools discussed here correspond to junior and senior high school, the students of the latter being mostly graduates of the former in the same system. Grade in school is obviously not an exact way of indicating who is adolescent and who is not, but since the students who are probably pre-adolescent and adolescent are largely found in these grades, they are the grades we shall study. (Even if we had an exact definition and measures to tell us who is or is not an adolescent, it would be unnatural for students as well as administratively clumsy and disruptive to screen all students.)

We know, secondly, that part of the process of growing up is the development of differences between the sexes, and so we shall try to discover whether or how the sexes differ in their attitudes toward school. We can carry this concern one step farther and, as our third goal, try to learn whether the kind or strength of attitudes, if they are different in the two sexes, are dependent

upon what grade ("stage" of adolescence) one is talking about.
(In the language of statistics, do the two variables interact?)
    Fourth, it would seem from general observation and specifical-
ly from the work of Coleman (1968, p. 18) that the attitudes
students have toward school will be related to kinds of attitudes
fellow students in a particular school have. Coleman writes in
terms of the background of fellow students, but it seems reasonable to examine the more generally stated notion that the quality
of a school should be related to attitudes toward it. Quality of a
school is an expression I shall not try to be very exact about,
since what is good in one community may not be altogether appropriate in another. Nevertheless, in order to draw distinctions
among the school systems studied here, I shall refer to variables
which tend to reflect the socioeconomic makeup of the community and both the inputs and outputs of the schools. "Good"
schools are expensive, and although an affluent community does
not necessarily have good schools, affluence can help.

Questions Not Studied

    There is simply a multitude of interesting questions to be found
nested within the general question, What attitudes do adolescents
have toward school? But time and resources dictated that they be
left to other studies. For example, to judge by the number of
"underground" newspapers (and books about them), there are
a good many students who are more radical or critical of school
than would appear from "above-ground" school publications or
newspaper reports. This opinion is firmly reinforced by parts of
the book by Gross and Osterman (1971). The details of the attitudes of the most radically critical subgroup of students toward
school would be a matter of both interest and illumination to
those who wonder why such groups of students exist. Similarly,
we may be very sure that in every school system there are students
who have been "turned off" but who have not yet dropped out,
because of parental pressure or the desire to remain with their
friends. Identifying and studying them as a subgroup might provide important information about what causes the turning off.
Equally important would be the study of how the relations between student and parent, and especially the expectations or re-

quirements of the latter, bear upon the student's attitudes toward school. From conversations with many people, including school psychologists and directors of guidance, I am sure this is a matter of vital importance but one sufficiently private in character, in the view of some officials and many parents, that in order to be allowed to work in the schools at all, I simply did not try to get at this factor. The inferences I can make from conversations I shall report in appropriate places, however, simply to provoke thought on this problem.

It certainly matters to a teacher who must face a class of 15 or 30 very different personalities that their attitudes vary and vary for different reasons, but, for reasons that will shortly become apparent, we are here restricted to statements about average attitudes in particular groups. At least we may be able to suggest to school staff members and parents some of the variations in attitude that clearly occur in general, and we may help the teacher or others note which statements made as generalizations do not fit particular students they deal with every day.

Perhaps the most general way of expressing what concerns us in Part 1 is to say we are concerned about the "match" between adolescent attitudes toward or related to school, on the one hand, and, on the other, what we know about the school as a place, a system, a social organization, in which they are involved for many hours each week for much of the year. In Part 2 we shall report the studies from which the analysis of the match stems.

We turn now to the question of how well the adolescent (that mythical "average" adolescent) fits the school, or, conversely, how well the school fits him. Substantiating data will be reported in Part 2, and while they in the main come from my own studies I shall not be reluctant to draw upon the studies or interpretations of others.

Identity

We said earlier that adolescence is a time of search for selfhood. That is, the adolescent seeks to learn "who he is," i.e., what *are* his values; what *is* he going to live for; where *does* he stand on significant questions; who *are* the people who make a difference to him, and why; how *is* he going to get along with those—whether remote or close, whether by the roles assigned them by society or by relationship to him—who have the power to influence his life?

I shall limit myself to commenting on one aspect of the conventional school which seems to me to be related in an obvious way to the search for identity. This is the curriculum, about which the student typically has little to say unless he is a "good" student in junior or senior years, and even then state law or local custom or resources may not permit a wide range of choice. The main point concerning the curriculum found in schools I have studied is that most of it is irrelevant to the important search for identity. It is instead devoted primarily to what are regarded as fundamentals, such as the mastery of mathematical, verbal, and writing skills. If the student has humanities-oriented studies, is able to get beyond the rote and the dull in that part of the curriculum and is given freedom to explore a range of literatures, he may be helped to think about some of the possible beings he might become.

Most of the rest of the curriculum is presently knowledge-oriented and skill-oriented. I call particular attention to what the social studies include. History is one of the most visible subjects, but it is likely to be difficult to make relevant to the lives

of students concerned about who they are, here and now, and
what they are becoming. Government, economics, and related
subjects have the disadvantage, unless taught in an especially
skillful way, of seeming remote and abstract. So I shall suggest
what is being done increasingly across the country: study of personality, development, interpersonal relations, adolescence, culture, social organization, and so on, and the existing social problems to which they relate, are being recognized as much more
likely to enable the adolescent, especially when he is given some
freedom, to steer his reading and discussion to the greatest concerns he has. This should be done throughout adolescence, i.e.,
should not take place too late, as a senior elective. Given competent teaching—and this is a big supposition—the study of such
topics might even legitimize discussion of such topics as sexuality
or drug abuse. I fully realize the loaded character of such suggestions, but I do not see the average student as getting more than
platitudes from his elders and probably a good deal of misinforma-
tion from his peers on such subjects. So if the surging emotion
could be reduced in discussion of these or other problems the
adolescent is grappling with, and I must repeat, under competent
leadership, an enormous contribution might be made to his development.

In the process his learning would in part be more personal and
real and in part, even when it is not personal, more acceptable in
his view. Perhaps, then, indifference toward school would be
lessened and such important subjects as history would not "turn
off" so many students. I should like to emphasize strongly that
I am not talking about a "life adjustment" curriculum with all
the connotations that label implies to different critics of it.
Rather, I should like to say flatly that no cognitive (intellectual)
process occurs without participant motivational and emotional
content, so that to emphasize knowledge and skills as though
these could be independent of the other components is to create
a kind of curriculum and instruction which is specifically inappropriate to and in large measure irrelevant to the nature of the learner.

I might add that others have emphasized that affective learning
and the learning of interpersonal relationships, as well as self-
understanding, should be added to cognitive learning. (See Fan-

tini and Young 1970, chaps. 3 and 4; Weinstein and Fantini 1970;
Borton 1970, esp. pt. 2, or Heath 1971, esp. pt. 5.)

Autonomy

In the opening discussion, attention was called to the striving
of the adolescent for autonomy—the feeling he can make it on
his own, he can make his own decisions, he can control his own
life and is not dependent on or controlled by others. What have
we learned that pertains to this?

In the analysis of attitudes toward the school as a social system,
I can suggest seven specific factors which relate to autonomy in
adolescence. First, there evidently is little feeling among students
that they are free to make their own decisions. Second, students
feel that there are too many requirements and specifications set
by the school. Third, students do not at all appreciate the degree
of control which the school insists on maintaining over them.
Fourth, they perceive the school as not needing all the rules it
has, just to operate. Fifth, they think they are treated as being
all alike. I understand them as feeling there is little allowance for
the fact that as human beings they are unique, and of an age to
be particularly sensitive on this point. Fantini and Young (1970,
pp. 54-55) regard it as lip service only for most teachers and administrators who speak of individualizing instruction. Sixth,
older students especially, but the younger ones as well, do not
like the "pass system" used to regulate student movement in the
building or outside. I think they feel this is a petty business, especially for those old enough to drive cars, hold part-time jobs,
regulate their evenings and weekends, and so on. Seventh, scheduling is perceived as rather objectionably inflexible. The interesting thing is that this finding occurs in the only school system I
studied which has a modular scheduling plan in the high school;
according to indirect and not provable information which comes
to me, many students there simply regard the modular scheduling as one more way the school regulates them, rather than free-
ing them. It may make adults feel that school is being run more
effectively, but students do not see it doing much for them.

Doubting, questioning, testing

We have said that adolescence is a time for these activities. This will have to be discussed on the basis of observation and conversations with students, teachers, and others.

The modal (_not_ model) teacher, and administrator too, I suspect, seems to be one who thinks that he or she, as part of the teacher or administrator role perhaps, is the final and unchallengeable authority in an assigned role. Saying "I don't know; I'll have to find out" is by a great many teachers regarded as visible evidence of incompetence or lack of self-confidence, not to mention loss of face in the eyes of students. Further, even if a student has a question, he is not likely to be allowed much class time to push it toward a satisfactory answer. Teachers have their own objectives for a lesson, and these generally include getting at least a certain distance farther in the general plan of a course, so detours are risky. (See Holt 1969, pp. 47 ff.) As a related aspect of this same problem there is the question of how much the student is allowed or encouraged to participate in classroom discussion. It is the opinion of Flanders (1970, p. 101), after a good many years of analysis of classroom processes, that on the average the teacher will talk about 68 percent of the time, students about 20 percent, and the remaining time will be spent in silence or confusion. I would go further, on the basis of observation and conversation, and guess that the student participation is usually in response to teacher questions and rarely is of the free-flowing variety that would permit the student to bring up the kinds of personal questions we have referred to earlier. Things are even worse for the student if the teacher uses the unexpected question as a device for ensuring student control or attention.

The remarkable thing to me is that in spite of this, students tend on the average to like their teachers. I can only think, as I said before, that things have been going on like this for so many years that they would not expect any other behavior of teachers, and in the main they do not see it as offensive or restrictive. At least such teacher behavior allows them to be passive, uninvolved, if they wish. At the college level, it has often been my experience in the past, and to some extent even now, that when I do everything I can to open up a seminar and give students much control over it, some of them do not know how to handle the situation and are filled with anxiety because I refuse to tell them what to do next. Or they feel I am not taking proper responsi-

bility for the class. The matter is perhaps best summed up by a
quotation from John Dewey's *The Child and the Curriculum*
(cited in Silberman 1970, p. 363): "Familiarity breeds contempt,
but it also breeds something like affection. We get used to the
chains we wear, and . . . through custom we finally embrace what
first wore a hideous mien." So the most common situation in
school is not one in which the adolescent can or does do the kind
of doubting or questioning or testing he normally would like to
do.

School as a place to live   .

   In what appear to be typical suburban schools such as I have
studied, it seems to be plain that the school is not for now. I infer this from the massive indifference to school I find on the average. It may even be evident in the students' denial that they
dislike school (and one has to consider seriously the possibility
that they are indeed so indifferent to school that it would be in-
exact to say they *could* dislike it). The picture is complicated
somewhat by the evident conscientiousness which holds many
students to their schoolwork *now*, but rather well-clarified by
their concern about the relation of their schoolwork to the future. Indeed, as the student has probably always been told, school
is preparation for later life, if only because it is instrumental in
getting a job, being admitted to college or whatever. To those
who are unsuccessful in school, the section title "Schools Are
Bad Places for Kids" (Holt 1969, p. 15) is probably appropriate.
Those who are successful by school standards and are rewarded
for being in school see it primarily as the means by which to get
somewhere else, probably college. (It is unfortunate that only
recently have colleges begun changing their rules and curricula
and easing restrictions in recognition of their students' conten-
tion that colleges have been just as bad a place as high schools for
a human being to live.) The point is especially important with respect to the high school full of adolescents because they are people
just moving into the realization of what it is like to live, especially
as an adult lives, and all too many of them become alienated from
school because they do not see the worth of being part of the
school existence. (See especially Gross and Osterman 1971,
"What It's Like.")

Community and adolescent

We all know that for several years there has been a crisis of confidence in the school. This may be felt by a particular citizen or parent for any or several of a long list of reasons, but I shall mention only a few examples. For one thing, there may be unrealistically high expectations as to how much a school can do with or for students, especially when parents cannot or do not help. Also, there may be mistrust of the motives of the school, ranging from fears that it will teach the "wrong" thing by someone's standards to feelings that schools cost too much for what they accomplish. In this connection, Grambs (1965, p. 94) speaks of a widespread distrust of intellectualism in this country, which presumably is at least in part related to the kind of experiences people, including parents, have had in school. Or there may be sheer ignorance and failure of communication between school and parents. I think of at least two reasons for this. One is that schools do not take sufficient initiative in keeping the community informed about what they are doing except when they want more money or there is some kind of crisis, as over rules of dress and appearance, drug abuse, or vandalism. The other is that many teachers do not like to deal with parents, because this occurs (apart from the annual school visitation evening) only when there is a difficult situation concerning a student which must be discussed. In fact, this distaste has now become so marked that teacher-representation groups have begun to use "no meetings with parents" as a point of negotiation in arriving at new contract understandings with the school board, and not merely in inner-city schools. Probably the responsibility for disseminating information in a credible way and not in time of emotional storm lies with the school, as does contact with the community concerning more than a common interest in sports.

Next we might mention the belief, which more and more people are challenging, that schooling, more and better but of the same general kind we have had, is essential for everyone. Surely it is time to re-examine this idea.

Finally, we might make explicit what was implied above: in communities where there are official bargaining units representing teachers, there are usually at least some people who believe that teachers and their leaders are more interested in money than in their sons and daughters. In recent times a good many bond issues for schools have been voted down—presumably in good part by voters whose children are or have been in the schools of their community.

Now back to the adolescent. If he knows that his community or his parents are not enthusiastic about schools, why should *he* be? Or if his parents or other relatives are the type of "concerned citizen" criticizing some aspect of schooling, why should he defy them?

Changing the system to fit its student members better

Underlying what I have said previously is the assumption that
basic human nature changes slowly, this despite occasional sud-
den, even disturbing manifestations of that nature in recent
times. It therefore becomes my intention to look at the school
as through the eyes of the adolescent, to learn whether possibilities of change in that social system can be suggested, and what is
the likelihood of any suggested change encountering resistance.

I should add that after realizing the importance of trying to
understand the match of the school with the nature of adolescence, I have discovered that this approach is not entirely novel.
It was used to some extent by Grambs (1965, chap. 9), by Heath
(1967, chap. 13), alluded to by Coleman (1965, pp. 10-12), and
mentioned in relation to elementary education by Jackson (1968,
chap. 2). None of these authors focuses as specifically or in as
much detail on the problem of the match as does the present
work.

Identity and individuality

Although there is much outward or superficial conformity
among adolescents in clothing, speech, "in" behavior, and so on,
a much more significant aspect of being an adolescent is, as we
have said, the search for identity, which always means individuality to some extent. At least two aspects of what happens in the
school now are typically antithetical to the effort of the adolescent to be or feel like an individual.

First, let me mention the tracking system, which exists in
most schools beginning with the formation of reading groups in
the first grade. Herbert Thelen (1970, pp. 1-18) expresses a view
which goes beyond the usual administrative concern for grouping
students by ability so that they may be better taught (in adult
opinion). Thelen takes the position that the school is after all a
microcosm of society, in which all ability levels are found, and

that grouping students by ability is de facto segregation. In another place Thelen (1967, pp. 28-29) summarizes the results of
a very large number of comparisons of homogeneous and heterogeneous grouping and concludes that with respect to achievement,
there is simply no consistent or proven difference between the
two systems and, indeed, with respect to outcomes such as self-
perception, feelings of inferiority, mental health, etc., the evidence is scantier but shows heterogeneous grouping to be consistently superior. Others have pointed out (Clarizio et al. 1970,
pp. 507-21) that students vary in so many ways that grouping as
such is not so influential as is the way a teacher uses it, or the
way all the other factors besides ability are influenced or are influential in the classroom. It has been argued that the work of
the teacher would be much more difficult with a heterogeneous
group, but there are a good many teachers who do not think
there would be more work, who believe there are advantages to
the student in heterogeneous grouping, and who in any case feel
that teaching would be more interesting.

Apart from the students in the "top" track—usually thought
of as potential college material—and their parents, who probably
think any other placement or arrangement would result in poorer
education, there seems to be no defense for tracking except the
school's convenience (since there are so many students, they
have to be divided up somehow into smaller groups). It may be
true, under certain circumstances, that the effort to match
teachers with students they think they can teach would result
in a kind of grouping that would facilitate learning (Thelen 1967,
chap. 10), but this is not tracking in the ordinary sense. In fact,
were it not so complex to manage, it might be seen as a replace-
ment for tracking systems based on test and achievement scores.

But students are much aware of the usual tracking system.
They resent being classified by test scores and grades (which
certainly could be de-emphasized), and most of them, including
some in the top track, think of tracking as one of the inhumane
aspects of the school. There are a good many varieties of tracking systems, but it would seem that without homogeneous grouping the students would not be learning less than they do now,
and their feelings about school might well be improved. Heterogeneous grouping, it is often suggested, can permit teaching of

one student by another with salutary effects on both. I might add that being placed in a track below the top one is regarded by many students as demeaning and as a prior judgment by someone in authority that he is not as worthy a person as certain others. This can go so far as to become a self-fulfilling prophecy: they say I will not do well; I notice my failures; I develop a poorer opinion of myself. In adolescence, particularly, this could only be regarded as extremely undesirable. I conclude that tracking ought to be greatly de-emphasized.

Another way of frustrating the wish to move toward identity and individuality is evident in the teaching style and expectations of many classroom teachers. As authors like Silberman (1970, pp. 148-49 and elsewhere) point out, the tendency of many teachers is to utilize a lecturing or questioning procedure in which it is very clear that it is the teacher who is active and controlling and treating the class as a unit, and the student is expected to be docile, passive, and just like the other members of the group in his response to this kind of treatment.

There are, of course, sensitive, responsive teachers who pay attention to individual differences, who respond to the class reaction, who can tolerate or encourage individual reaction by students. I don't know where this kind of teacher behavior is taught, but the restrictive model tends ordinarily to have been fixed in the teacher by the way he or she was schooled at an earlier age. It probably becomes in part a defensive maneuver, and it is a rather unusual teacher who in maturity does not reflect this tendency. If teacher-training institutions pay insufficient attention to the problem, then those working with beginning teachers must attempt to do so. But there simply must be more emphasis on treating students as individuals.

As an aside I remark that those concerned about individualizing instruction effectively (e.g., Clarizio et al. 1970, pp. 522-33) do not necessarily see in the ungraded classroom system any assurance that there will be more effective attention to how one student differs from another, because so much depends upon how the teachers and administrators use or define "ungraded."

Autonomy and independence

The dominant theme in many classrooms, and in many administrator's offices, appears to be law and order first and then, if possible, learning. I mentioned earlier the negative attitudes of adolescents to rules, passes, and the other apparatus supposed to be conducive to maintaining order and conformity. And, despite the fact that in my studies students in general liked teachers, they sometimes did not like teacher behavior involved in management of the classroom. For example, students said they did not like teachers who keep strict control of the classroom. Furthermore, they thought many teachers overly quick to be suspicious of students. Yet they did not feel teachers were to be avoided because they were "too bossy." And, in fact, they did not feel what I claimed in a very general way above, namely, that teachers care more about keeping order and quiet than about whether their students learn. Evidently my generalized statement, however widely accepted, has to be qualified.

It seems more likely that it is administrators—who tend to evaluate teachers in considerable measure by how well they "control" or "manage" a class, and who make most rules about conduct in the school—who need to realize the consequences of the control approach. Every negative evaluation of a teacher I personally have seen has contained comment on this point. (It is often the only comment.) Interestingly enough, I have been told by several experienced school people with whom I have discussed this matter that even when an administrator is forced by circumstances to take over some particular problem of student conduct, there is great variability in what may happen. It appears that most administrators faced with this choose to play it tough, but there are some who try to counsel with the student, and still others who attempt to be a father figure. The main theme expressed by people who have told me this is that there is no training of administrators in this respect and, therefore, they usually do not develop an explicit policy which can be followed consistently.

Whatever the extent to which the law-and-order atmosphere prevails in a building, then, it would seem that four changes might be sought to relieve this kind of pressure on students. First there should be schoolwide consistency in the handling of disciplinary and other matters, within the limits set by the fact that human beings cannot perform with perfect consistency.

Next, and this suggestion has been tried with varying degrees of success in the past, perhaps because it has been just tinkering with part of the system and not dealing with the whole system, ways ought to be found of permitting students to influence the administration of discipline so that when discipline seems necessary, it will be tempered by student reaction and understood better by all who are involved. Again there is reason to think strongly that more respect for students and more trust in their capacity to regulate themselves will not only make them feel better about school but make teaching and administering less exhausting. And fourth, both inside the classroom and out, domination of student life by rules should be eased.

One thing is clear, however, and it is that the community knows, or thinks it knows, how things are run in school, and it is characteristic in this country to cry for repressive measures as the first reaction to a report of any misconduct. So change inside the building has to be carried out after informing and seeking the cooperation and understanding of those who are inclined to consider students immature and irresponsible. This will receive further discussion.

There simply was no opportunity in the research supporting the bulk of this report to assess student attitudes toward grading and evaluation. With respect to grading there is fair reason to think we know how most students feel. Except for the students who succeed easily on tests and get high grades, these aspects of school are disliked to a degree that approaches hatred and fear in some students. The fact that they are used as weapons in what some teachers perceive as the battle to contain students certainly does not make matters better. And the fact that they are used to classify or categorize, often not very fairly, and that parents often demand grade performance and even punish for failure to reach parental standards, likewise does not make the student any more accepting of the situation. So I repeat that tests and grades must somehow be de-emphasized for the good of learning.

In the usual case, grades are not used as evaluation devices. This matter has been discussed recently by Silberman (1970, esp. p. 347) and Holt (1964, pt. 1) and will not be discussed here in detail. (Their emphasis on how students "learn the teacher" rather than the subject in order to get the grade should be noted,

however.) Suffice it to say that grades are demanded with little
or no regard for either the consequences of using schooling as a
way of classifying people or for the evaluation which is far more
rare and important. In fact, evaluation is so rare that I perhaps
should state that by the term I mean privately informing the student, by any reasonable procedure, of his progress, his weak and
his strong points, or of anything else that has a bearing on how
he is doing and how he assesses himself. The prevalence of grades,
their use for tracking and other purposes, and the pressures from
employers, colleges, and parents to have indicators of how well
a student performs in school, mean they are going to be with us
for some time, and it is probably not realistic for now to urge
that they simply be abolished, as does Holt (1969, p. 32). But
much more that is constructive could be done with them, and
with additional information as well, for the information and guidance of the student. Probably much of the unpredictability or un-
reliability of grading policy could be removed by the school.
That would ease one more irritant to the student and perhaps
lend some positive value to the persisting practice.

Anxiety and guilt

In my observations it was clear that anxiety and guilt attitudes
with respect to school prevail among a significant proportion of
students. Needless to say, if the attitudes are strong and in significant degree truly school-related, this can hardly make school
a desirable place to be. Grades and tests, as ordinarily used, are a
potent source of anxiety, and it seems reasonable to suppose that
all the other possibilities of doing something wrong (against the
rules, that is) serve to maintain anxiety feelings in school. One
can even sense, by sitting in a school front office, that the clerks
and secretaries there regard the students as objects that come and
go, not as people with their own concerns and, in a good many
cases, anxieties. Being treated as a "nothing" could hardly be re-
assuring.

Anxiety and guilt presumably do not start in school, but rather
at home before the child starts school. So the real question is,
Can teachers and administrators be made sensitive to this problem and do what they can at least to prevent exacerbating it?
Some of the behaviors that ordinarily prevent anxiety from in-

creasing can be named, and, it is hoped, be improved. Reducing the unpredictability of any aspect of school is one (this is not the same thing as becoming inflexible). Freely giving reasons or explanations as to why something is to be done, and how, with what objectives, not only makes for better teaching and administration but makes the whole situation less to be concerned about. If students can be given a share of responsibility for decision making of certain kinds, in a manner that shows it is a real responsibility and not one to be snatched back if some school staff member does not really approve, they are likely to feel better about what they do. In general, supportiveness, not restrictiveness, is helpful. Again we have to remark that concern for this sort of thing does not seem to be a part of teacher-preparation curricula, or teacher selection, so that the pattern will have to be set and the skills acquired when new teachers come into a building. The administrators and teachers who are already there will, in many cases, have to change their ways of dealing with students and new teachers, and whether parents can be made to understand the problem and, in general, be cooperative is a question still to be answered.

I should perhaps add that it would not be appropriate to think that ideally all anxieties should somehow be removed. There is a necessity for certain anxieties or fears to protect us against possible harm, and in school it is likely to be the case that even the successful student who has no basic anxiety about school will nevertheless at least be concerned, just because he cares about school.

Social distractibility

A very real challenge exists in the fact that students are responsive to their friends in school as well as out (although Douvan and Adelson [1966, p. 344] feel that peer-group pressures have been exaggerated). But at the present time the only real way a keen interest in one's peers is legitimized in school is in extracurricular activities. In fact, I use the heading social distractibility because of my belief that most school staff members regard time spent with friends as time wasted with respect to schooling.

Oddly enough, it may be useful to set aside the idea of social distractibility as such and approach the matter from a different

direction. Coleman (1961, p. 318) points out that a student who
does well in school (gets high marks) by definition is putting
other students down, a thing that not many students like to do.
The clearest case in which competitiveness is good is that of
athletics. There, the better the individual does, the better off his
team is and the more admired and honored he is.

As Coleman
suggests, competitiveness is going to continue to exist, but in
friendship groups outside school it is regulated in one manner or
another so that friends can remain friends. The motivation is without doubt strong in many students, but the school has thus far
found no way to make clearly good use of it in aid of learning.
It shows up primarily in connection with grade-getting, and so
many school people have felt the effects to be undesirable that
competitiveness has been de-emphasized over the last several
decades, and efforts have been made to draw upon other kinds
of motivation.

But our society demands classification, via grades, I.Q. scores,
or other indicators, so the school can't successfully play down
all the evils of competition and must instead try to find ways of
using it constructively. As things presently stand, competing
against one another for grades in school is just one more aspect
of having to do one's duty there, rather than liking it. Probably
the only long-run solution for this will finally have to be Goodman's (1962, p. 154) radical one: if schools ceased to give grades,
it would become safe and legitimate for a student to be cooperative with one's peers, or for peers to teach one another, and the
teacher would not be in the position of being that person who
hands out grades and therefore someone not to be fully liked.
Goodman's position is shared by Melby (1966, p. 104) and many
others. Again, I realize the controversial nature of the suggestion
for the typical school and community, but I know of no one who
as yet has found an easier way to let adolescents live in peace
with their peers in school.

One can find a somewhat more optimistic description of the
possibilities of taking advantage of the strong interest students
have in other students in Bronfenbrenner's _Two Worlds of Childhood: U.S. and U.S.S.R._ (1970, pp. 155-58). After a discussion
of U.S. child-rearing and schooling practices, he makes a number
of suggestions about how to utilize student interests and friend-

ships. Apart from modifying classroom composition in terms of social class and race, he believes that other powerful forces can be put to work. For example, he mentions the psychological identification by students, not merely with selected adults, but with particular peers; he mentions the use of reinforcements (rewards, etc.) from peers as well as adults; there is the possibility of group commitment to certain goals, i.e., those which lie above or beyond the immediate situation with its many temptations to self-aggrandizement. He believes change may be possible through inventiveness in the use of teams, cooperative group competition (Coleman formulated a comparable idea), organized patterns of mutual help, including in the mutual-help groups mixes of race, social class, sex, achievement, and the like. He suggests the possibility of two-student learning teams composed of students of heterogeneous ability. Above all, he would like to see the involvement of pupils in responsible tasks on behalf of others within the classroom, the school, the neighborhood, and the community (p. 156). While these suggestions might require adaptation or, as said, inventiveness, they do suggest that motivating students by other than internalized (originally externally demanded) competitiveness is possible. In this I find cause for hope.

Evaluation of change

One of the greatest shortcomings of research or efforts to change things in universities or schools in the past is that no way of evaluating the effect or outcome is planned. As students of the process of change are aware, it is necessary to know before any change is made just how a system is functioning. Then measures have to be made after the change has had time to have an effect to see whether any effect has occurred, and, if so, whether it is favorable or merely an artifact of novelty. There are many technical and practical problems here, but as I said about attitude change, anyone who wishes to introduce change had better familiarize himself with these problems, and with the concept of control groups of various kinds to assess the influence of factors other than the intended change.

It is one of the very great drawbacks of educational and other research or program funding that the money often comes with a time limit attached. As a result, before there can be proper plan-

ning for pre-evaluation, the change is introduced and that makes
impossible an adequate postevaluation. (As an important
example of this, see the Westinghouse Learning Corporation-
Ohio University study, *The Impact of Head Start,* 1969.) The
accountability principle is vaguely understood, but not necessarily
the conditions by which adequate information may be gathered
to ascertain just what has been accomplished by the introduction
of programs or by research.

Obstacles to Change

Let us consider further how difficult it is to change the school,
despite the fact that hundreds of tinkering jobs have already been
done and some major changes made. The major recent work on
the problem of change is that by Sarason (1971). The most interesting and recent changes, as reported by Silberman (1970, chap.
8), have been reconstructions of the whole concept of a high
school, in which much emphasis is laid on freedom and self-determination by students. The experiments have had to be done
outside the regular school system in several cases, although in
one case an entire new program for a city high school was planned
in advance by a group of graduate students in education who, after getting their degrees, were hired as a group to put into action
thoroughly innovative plans which they had been discussing during their days as graduate students. Since those experiments are
described elsewhere and are not ready for evaluation, I shall leave
it to the interested reader to read Silberman and other authors
(such as Gross and Gross 1969) for the nature of the innovations.

It is ironic that Theodore R. Sizer finds cause to remark (in Brownell 1972, pp. 8-9) that it has been much easier to introduce reform
at the primary school level than at the secondary. In his view
people do not really think the primary schools are very important but secondary schools can have important consequences, so
that change from the status quo is viewed with alarm.

A very concrete obstacle to change in the schools is that change
always carries with it some uncertainty as to outcome or some
initial student over-reaction, and some change in the way students
or staff operate. Hence it is threatening to administrators, teachers,
and others. On the other hand, I have known of teachers who

wished to change some aspect of what they were doing and felt they dared not do so because it would be upsetting to administrators, or to teachers who would have the students later on, for that matter, in another period of the day. Fortunately, if you talk to an effective administrator, there is a good chance that you will find him saying that any teacher proposing almost any reasonable change will be told to try it and "more power to you." This suggests that intraschool communication may often be poor. In general, we must agree with Cottle (1967, esp. chap. 8) that teachers, administrators and others who attempt to produce change are very vulnerable to forces within and without the school.

Another obstacle to change is to be found in the attitudes of parents. Most of them attended authoritarian schools, and they expect the schools to keep students "in line." Too often the first and unthinking response to suggestions for change is negative, so that, as mentioned before, parents must be brought in on discussions of any decisions about changes in the schools. It is frustrating to the administrator or teacher who wishes to communicate with parents to find that so many of them do not want to put out the time or the energy; they merely wish the school to educate their children while they are doing other things. Grambs (1965, p. 27), as we have said, develops the idea that experience has made many parents basically anti-intellectual. The effect of this on their children seems easy to predict.

We need only mention here the attitudes of nonparents who are nevertheless taxpayers and who have their own opinions of the schools and the students. Establishing useful communication with them on issues in which they have a legitimate interest is both necessary and difficult.

A good many of the problems we have discussed earlier might be alleviated by changes in teacher-preparation programs. Particularly, from the point of view of a psychologist, there ought to be more emphasis on human relations, since that is what schooling is about as much as subject matter or skills. I should make it clear that I mean by emphasizing human relations not simply how to control students more effectively, but how to bring it in as a school curriculum component, as well as making it an overriding concern of all those involved in the school. But one has only to talk to a beginning teacher to find that no matter where that person was trained, he or she feels inadequate to the task of dealing with a group of 20 or 30 young people all at once, not often with respect to subject matter, but usually with respect to the interactions among students and interactions of students and teacher.

Related to this is the inclination to think of preparation for teaching primarily in terms of curriculum, teaching machines, formats (such as team teaching), or methods (usually in relation to certain subject matter). Such thinking, of course, has its use, and changes are being made all the time (but usually they are not evaluated, so the effect of the change is unknown). As is by now very clear, I myself am inclined to think first of the students in the school, and how the schooling they receive might be adapted to the kinds of people they are. I believe this offers the most important possibility for meaningful change in the near future, and it does not require much extra expenditure of money.

But I must repeat that changing any aspect of a school involves aspects of the whole organization, and it and the people who make it up must all be considered simultaneously. Attitude change is central to the whole process. Attitudes *must* be dealt with.

PART 2:
EMPIRICAL STUDIES

5. CHOOSING A METHOD

In discussing briefly the work of previous investigators of adolescents in school, I alluded to their use of questionnaires, interviews, and other procedures. I have mentioned Coleman's use of questionnaires plus informal interviews; Erikson's work based largely on psychoanalysis; Keniston's use of interviews, psychological tests, and other procedures; and the work of Friedenberg and his associates employing interviews and various ingenious questionnaire-type instruments. I could equally well have mentioned the work of Douvan and Adelson (1966, preface), who took considerable pains to ensure that the interview would not be too intensely personal and felt that the young people interviewed were open and candid in their replies (although they used an interviewing service which sampled across the nation, and it seems to me that it might be difficult to arrive at an evaluation of candidness under such circumstances). In any event, to plan for their interviews it was necessary that a good many questions be essentially projective in intent, so that the question arises as to how adequately their interpretations of replies might be made. The insight of psychoanalysts may come closer to the truly personal sense of growing up, but there we encounter the problem of sample size and representativeness that is part of the natural life of a clinical researcher.

My own preliminary experiences made me very sensitive about two matters. The first was that anyone, stranger or not, who wishes to secure reasonably accurate information about anything an adolescent considers his private business faces a difficult problem, especially if the investigator is perceived as snooping and particular adolescents are the object of this nosiness. (Friedenberg and his collaborators [in Nordstom et al. 1967, pp. 141 ff.] are much concerned about closely related points.) The second matter about which I developed concern was sampling. Adolescents, I should assume, are as different from one another as any group defined by any other criterion. This means that drawing a sample of some defined kind from the available adolescents in the school runs many risks, not merely of bias with respect to whatever one is studying but of not including individuals who would, as a hoped-for bonus, provide information which one had not set out to find in the first place. Careful sampling would also be a nuisance to everyone who participated in it. As a reaction to this second concern, I decided that my strategy would call for entire-school populations in the grades I worked with. This turned out to be fortunate, for I began with three school systems, which I shall describe later, and was both puzzled by certain results and edified by the students' freehand comments; as a consequence the range of my reading and conversations with my own students and colleagues were extended, and I felt forced to make a change in procedure (not an enormous one, to be sure) and then include a fourth school system.

With respect to the matter of privacy, it has always seemed to me that in school the student is likely to be careful about what he says to whom, because school is seen by him as a place where it is rather easy to get into trouble for saying the wrong thing. More than this, adolescents who live within reasonable commuting distance of a university are likely to have found perfect strangers studying them often enough that they may not be willing to cooperate unless it is clear that something worthwhile is being done and that it is safe to be cooperative. In the fourth school system in which I gathered data, there were seemingly a few students who felt antagonistic to further investigations (or perhaps to school), and as I shall discuss this school separately it will be necessary to raise the question of how unintended sampling bias through refusals to carry out the task may have affected the results.

In the studies reported here every effort was made, short of the ludicrous, to assure students that their right to privacy would be fully respected (which meant, incidentally, that they could not be identified as individuals for other types of data-gathering). For example, anonymous questionnaires were used to gather information, despite the fact that there are obvious reasons to be concerned about the dependability of information so gathered. No interview or other procedures permitting student identification were used. It happened to be possible in all the school systems studied to have teachers administer the questionnaire during either a homeroom period or a special period set by the principal so that every student in a building gave his reactions during the same time period. Since more than one building was involved in each school system, if the identical hour was not available everywhere, the questionnaires were administered in the second (and in one instance, the third) building that same day so that discussions among or with students in the first building at lunch or other times would not influence the responses of students who had not yet had the questionnaire.

Each teacher had a copy of the questionnaire in advance, so that it, and especially the cover page of instructions to the student, could be studied and the teacher prepared to answer questions about the instructions *only*. When the students entered the room and the questionnaires were distributed, the first sentence they saw on the cover page was "Please do not write your name on this paper." The students were asked to read the cover page of instructions carefully and to ask for clarification if needed. Questions, it turned out, were extremely infrequent because the task and the instructions were so simple. When the teacher was sure each student was satisfied he understood the instructions, he or she was supposed to remind the students not to skip the first line on the first page of the questionnaire (which asked for grade, sex, and some information irrelevant to the research such as the student's age), then retire to a place in the room where obviously no student's responses could possibly be seen. When everyone had finished, a student collected the papers and took them to a designated place in the building and merely reported the room or division identification so that a clerk or secretary could be sure all papers had come in.

In addition, cooperating teachers and administrators were reminded in writing of the high desirability of student anonymity, if the research were to succeed. Also, the instructions to the students (see appendix A) emphasized anonymity rather strongly. There of course is no way of telling whether this rather conspicuous effort to protect the individual student in whatever he wished to say did in fact encourage valid responses. However, as will appear later, the measurements made seemed reliable enough for our purposes, as evaluated statistically, and beyond this, the internal consistency of the results suggests that most of the time lawfulness is being revealed which presumably could not be the case if, say, a goodly proportion of the students were deliberately falsifying responses. In addition, a surprising number of students voluntarily wrote such statements as "I enjoyed this!" or "Why don't we do this kind of thing more often?" and some teachers reported quiet chuckles or delighted looks on student faces. All this suggests the students found the task acceptable, in the main, so there is no obvious reason to disbelieve any large number of responses. Only in the fourth school system, as I have indicated, were there more than very rare refusals to cooperate.

Some History and the Present Formulation of the Problem

My interest in attitudes toward school began, as is often the case, in a somewhat different area, that of attempting to construct new measures of strength of motivation to achieve well in school. Most of that work was based on data gathered in England on a year's leave from my own university. Back in this country, I decided there were two main flaws in my English work. One was that I had asked students to respond to questions or statements that were based on my own personal observations in many classrooms, and I did not really understand the subtleties of English school situations. Also, I *did* ask for names on the questionnaires, and I have already indicated the possible flaw thus introduced. So, to begin work at the "grass roots" in my own country, I asked experienced teachers in a high school and a junior high to meet with me and to help me by writing down the signs by which they could tell when a student was strongly or weakly motivated with respect to his schoolwork. Either the teachers were not accustomed to this kind of analytical thinking (this does not imply an insult, for I could readily imagine an experienced teacher would be able to make judgments about students but no longer be able to tell exactly why the opinion was what it was), or I failed to make my request understandable. Whatever the explanation, they mostly sat and stared at their blank papers. I then thought that perhaps my presence or the presence of other teachers inhibited thought, so I explained what I sought to another group of high school teachers, provided them with a special sheet of paper with statements to remind them of the nature of my request, plus a self-addressed envelope, and closed the meeting. Even when they were reminded of the request by means of a note from the principal, not more than a handful responded.

Finally my difficulties in getting teacher opinions began to intrigue a teacher of English. He apparently had personally found the task a difficult one. So he gathered together a number of teacher friends and they spent an evening first discussing, then writing. Once they got under way, they were able to come up with a fairly long list of suggested indicators which various members of the group depended upon in judging strength of motivation in their students. When I received them I began writing up the indicators in the form of statements which a student might later be asked to rate as to how true any one was of him. The more thoroughly I studied the indicators and the statements I was producing, the more apparent it became that my original concern for achievement motivation was far too narrow. What informed and influenced the teacher reactions was a much broader range of student reactions, whether verbal or in other forms. It was at that point I became convinced of the necessity of studying a wide variety of student reactions to and in school. My ideas *had* to be reformulated, so that the detection and measurement of attitudes of various kinds became the problem.

Although a fairly straightforward academic definition of the word attitude was given earlier, it is desirable to hold two aspects of that definition in mind. The first is that if one limits the scope of applicability of any particular definition in order to be clear and specific, one runs the risk of missing the central theme of *the* attitude. On the other hand, in trying to define an attitude in such a way as to capture its complexities or intricacies, one runs the risk of including so much that just what *is* the central theme becomes ambiguous. My first reaction to this problem was to let the students themselves tell me just what were their attitudes toward school, i.e., what were the dimensions along which they might have a negative, indifferent, or a positive attitude. Considerable work was wasted in this effort, and it is reported briefly here so that anyone else attempting to approach the problem this way will be aware of some of the difficulties.

First a questionnaire consisting of 100 statements, based mainly on suggestions by the teachers referred to previously and edited by high school students meeting with me as a group, was administered anonymously to grades 7 through 12 in two school systems. The students circled a number for each statement between +3 (very true of me) and -3 (very untrue of me), with 0 as the indifference point in a row of numbers. (See appendix A for the format but not the exact list of statements.) Then the technique of factor analysis was to be applied. Under appropriate conditions this quite precise statistical procedure will indicate, among a heterogeneous set of questions or statements, those which correlate well with each other but not with members of other clusters. From a study of these clusters of statements, one infers what general meaning they have in common, and the cluster, given some brief label (such as an aspect of attitude toward school which all statements touch on in their various ways), is thereafter identified as a factor. In later work the statements may be revised, deleted, or new ones added, but the intent is to keep or clarify the general core of meaning which brought out the factor in the first place.

Examination of my exploratory data disclosed several features which made me doubt that the answers students gave to the various statements could or should be intercorrelated. First, in almost any population, the strength of any measured attitude is likely to be distributed unevenly across the available range of expression (here, a seven-step scale). Responses of different students tend to push toward the negative end of the scale or to pile up at the positive end, or at both. Rarely is an attitude (if indeed it *is* an attitude that is being evaluated) expressed with indifference by very many raters. Unfortunately, for the computation of a correlation coefficient, regardless of the particular kind of coefficient being used, it is assumed that the scores on any two variables being correlated are distributed as to frequency of responses at various points along each scale in a reasonably close approximation to the "normal" curve. Nevertheless, since I intended to try factor analysis and the intercorrelations were but a kind of preliminary arithmetic, they were computed. (I might say here that I consulted several statisticians about this matter and was encouraged to go ahead with both this step and the factor analysis. They pointed out that, after all, if the results made sense and could be repeated from one batch of data to another, one need not worry unduly about the adequacy of the assumptions made during the computations.)

A second difficulty arises when there are only seven steps discernible along each of the variables being correlated. (This is referred to as "restriction of range.") Having several more steps along each variable makes it possible to secure more discriminating information and provides a better chance of learning accurately just how large the correlation is. This problem had been anticipated during the decision to use the seven-step scale, and the reasoning went about as follows. The judgment of the intensity of one's own attitudes is at best rather difficult if refined judgments are required. It was felt that students as young as, say, seventh-graders, probably could not cope with an eleven-step scale. On the other hand, even a younger student can surely judge more than whether his attitude is positive or negative (if it is other than indifferent). This finally led to the decision to assume that, if he were not indifferent (0 on the scale) the student could tell the direction (plus or minus) of his attitude, and he could also characterize it as very strong, moderately strong, or not very strong (3, 2, or 1). Hence, I used the seven-step scale (+3 to −3) despite its probable shortcoming as discussed above. I might note that a study of the reliability and validity of comparable rating scales by Matell and Jacoby (1971, pp. 657-74) indicates that the number of steps in the scale, in their study as well as those by others, is not a highly significant matter.

Third, in all ratings there is the possibility of momentarily erratic thought, leading to inaccuracy of a particular response. If this seems an important possibility, the researcher usually tries to increase the number of statements rated, hoping that error will cancel out. But in the present case it was simply a fact of school life that the number of statements rated could not be increased as much as one might wish because a class period is only so long and because many classes contain some slow readers or judges. In addition, it would have been unreasonable or impossible to demand an additional period from the whole school.

As one might expect from the preceding discussion, the intercorrelations of the 100 statements, each with all the others separately, were quite variable and most of them were not very large. It was statistically possible, of course, to factor-analyze the intercorrelations to determine which ones clustered together and to examine the factors to determine whether they appeared to reflect an attitude of this or that kind toward school. But, to make a long story short, no single factor analysis could be replicated exactly no matter how similar the second group was on which the analysis was tried. The final blow came when the twelfth-grade boys of a single school were divided randomly in half and their questionnaire responses factor-analyzed separately. Several factors appeared in the two groups which bore much resemblance to one another, but various statements popped up in different factors in the two analyses. To complete this record of failure, multidimensional scaling followed by cluster analysis also came to grief in the same way, but I shall not take further space to discuss those problems of statistical technique. The data simply were not suitable for these precision methods of analysis, and it therefore was not possible to start without preconceptions and let the students themselves, through their anonymous responses, indicate what kinds of attitudes toward school were reflected in their reactions.

6. THE CHOSEN METHOD AND THE SCHOOLS
IN WHICH IT WAS USED

My studies were originally intended to include three school systems; I later added a fourth school system to the study. This chapter and the two following pertain to the original three systems (hereafter referred to as School A, School B, and School C); chapter 9 describes the work in the fourth system (School D), together with the necessary remarks about the minor but seemingly important changes that were made in the measurements and the manner in which they were made.

Although, as the preceding section showed, it is not as yet possible to start with a clean slate upon which the students themselves write the names of the different kinds of attitudes which they may possess toward school, it is not necessary to make altogether blind guesses about what these attitudes may be. One can talk with students, at random or in some preplanned interview style; if one is a parent he overhears his children and their friends talking about school; there is a considerable literature about personality development and about adolescence; there is the opportunity to discuss such matters with teachers and administrators; and there is a most informative source in college students studying psychology, for they understand the problem one is interested in and remember vividly their own attitudes toward events, persons, and arrangements in school. It gradually became apparent to me that I confronted a special problem here, for most students who can get into Yale were academically at or near the top of any school they ever attended and were likely to have been rewarded often, given special privileges, and so on. Thus one has to attempt to sort out what they actually experienced from what they now experience in fantasy, and both of these from what they observed happening to or among other students in their schools, especially the ones in slower groups. Beyond these sources of information, of course, my preliminary but never technically satisfactory work was very suggestive.

Convinced that simpler methods of analysis were necessary if

I were to make progress toward the assessment of attitudes toward school, I adopted a familiar strategy. I simply composed scales for measurement of the direction and strength of attitudes which information gleaned from sources like those mentioned in the previous paragraph led me to believe did exist. I am sure there are many, many more attitudes and that my scales could be shown to measure not just one but a combination of subtly different attitudes, but one can go only so far in one step. I created seven scales, and I shall now describe how this was done.

On the basis of the earlier factor analyses, I was fairly sure of what four of the scales should attempt to measure. Since my preliminary work had suggested that about 100 statements were all that could be handled by students in a typical classroom period, I decided I could create three more scales. Thus a total of seven scales, each including 14 statements, would constitute the questionnaire. The intended "core of meaning" for each attitude scale was decided subjectively. As before, the individual student responded to each statement by circling a number in the range from +3 (very true of me) to –3 (very untrue of me). The seven scales are shown in appendix B. They are intended to measure these more or less arbitrarily named attitudes: positive and active liking for school; generalized dislike of school; conscientiousness; anxiety and guilt about school; favorable attitude toward teachers; social distractibility; and orientation toward the future. The reason not all scales finally contained 14 statements will be explained shortly.

It should be remembered throughout that such an approach to the measurement of attitudes is purely descriptive and in a literal sense does not permit one to draw conclusions about why any datum is what it is. The temptation to wonder about this, i.e., to think in causal terms, is nevertheless almost overpowering at times, and so I shall, under the label of speculation, occasionally comment on how certain findings might be understood. But, I repeat, no manipulations were performed, no controls were available to check on the correctness of such speculations, and they must for now remain merely that.

To avoid negative numbers for computer work and for presentation of results here, +4 was added to whatever number the student circled. Thus the indifference point (0) on the scale indicating strength of attitude became 4; 7 indicated a very strong attitude (a statement very true of the student responding) and 1 was at the opposite extreme. A good many of the statements were more naturally or easily written in negative wording. If this fact would lead to the student's circling a number which meant psychologically the opposite of his real attitude, the scoring was reversed so that his position made psychological sense. For example, if a student circled +3 (very true of me) with respect to the statement that "Teachers put too much emphasis on learning facts and not on what they mean, in my opinion," he is psychologically communicating his displeasure with teachers. His answer, therefore, would be reversed to –3. Then +4 was added to it, so that he would receive a 1 to indicate the far opposite from 7, a very favorable attitude toward teachers.

Although 14 statements were included originally in each scale in the questionnaire, after the data were collected in each school system an item-analysis was made of each scale to determine whether, when all the data were in, all 14 items seemed to belong in the scale as intended. This was done by correlating the response to each individual item with the median of all the other reactions to statements in a given scale, and the procedure was repeated within the 12 subgroups (6 grades, 2 sexes) being studied in each school system. Because most of the subgroups were fairly large, a correlation coefficient did not have to be very large to be fairly significant in the statistical sense, and so it was decided to use a fairly severe criterion by which to decide whether to keep or discard a statement from a scale. This criterion was "not more than two correlations (in the 12 subgroups) between a statement and the median on the remaining statements of the scale below the .05 level of significance." (See p. 57 for explanation of "level of significance.")

Since the subgroups in two of the three school systems were rather large, a correlation of only about .15 between a statement and the median of the remainder of the statements in a presumed scale would reach the .05 level. Hence, it may be worth reporting that in School A, which had the largest number of students, in any subgroup the numbers of actual statement-scale correlations of .45 or higher were: for positive and active liking for school, 129 out of a possible 168 (14 statements, 12 subgroups); for generalized dislike of school, 89 out of a possible 156 (13 statements); for conscientiousness, 136 out of 168; for anxiety and guilt, 102 out of 156; for favorable attitude toward teachers, 51 out of 132 (11 statements); for social distractibility, 56 out of 132; and for orientation toward the future, 79 out of 156. A considerable number of the correlations were in the .50s, .60s, and even the .70s. Of the statement-scale correlations which did not reach the highly significant level of .45, it is clear on inspection of the tally charts that the great bulk are higher than .30, so that the coherence of the items retained in each scale is quite clear. The tallies for Schools B and C were similar. (Wherever possible, the initial computations were based on the subgroups, to avoid misjudgments that could result from using total-school data and being overly impressed with the statistical results one can get from very large numbers of cases.)

To create the 98-statement questionnaire of appendix A, I went through each scale assigning each statement a number from 1 to 98 by using a table of random numbers, with the restriction that at least two statements from other scales had to be between any two from a given scale. (This turned out to be impossible in a few instances, so that two statements from a given scale thus have but one statement from another scale between them.)

By a stroke of good fortune and a little "fudging," exactly the same statements could be retained for use in the three school systems to be discussed here. The fudging mentioned means that in School C two additional items could have been retained in one of the scales by the criterion spelled out on page 43, but they were discarded anyway, so that exactly the same instruments of measurement were used to obtain all data analyzed. Thus the scales presented in appendix B are the final forms for these three schools and include a total of 89 rather than 98 statements. Item analysis eliminated 1 item from the scale measuring generalized dislike of school, 1 from the anxiety-guilt scale, 3 from the liking-for-teachers scale, 3 from the social distractibility scale, and 1 from the orientation-toward-the-future scale.

Earlier, reference was made to the fact that responses to statements about attitude typically are not distributed in a group of reasonably homogeneous persons in any approximation of the "normal" curve. This is equally true for the responses of a single individual to the statements of a particular scale, for the various statements he rates as to their degree of truth for him personally do not all strike him in exactly the same way. This became self-evident when the computer was required to print out the exact point on the seven-step scale at which an individual student rated each statement as to how true it was of him. (In fact, this analysis was made in Schools A, B, and C for the first fifty students in each subgroup for each of the seven scales.)

As an example, let us consider two students who, by a measure to be mentioned later, come out at exactly the same scale position on the scale purporting to measure positive and active liking for school.

	Number circled by student 7016	Number circled by student 7011
If I have questions about something I have read outside class, I always try to bring them up in class.	4	5
I very much like to help the teacher with classroom chores, such as moving furniture, giving out papers, or cleaning the board.	1	5
I very much enjoy learning new words.	6	5
I think it's interesting to pull together all the different things I learn in one course or class.	6	3
If a classroom discussion gets confused, I feel I ought to help get things straightened out.	7	5
I like very much to be with good students.	5	5

If I see how to help a teacher plan or do something better, I am quick to suggest it.	3	6
Some subjects interest me so much that I read a lot more about them than is required.	7	5
I like school and I like learning.	5	5
I get a lot out of classroom discussions.	2	5
I enjoy inventing or suggesting projects for work in school.	4	3
I never get bored in class.	1	6
I really like clubs or activities connected with school subjects that interest me.	5	7
It feels good to understand something fully.	7	7

As indicated above, these examples could be extended for hundreds more students on each of seven scales. As one scans this mass of data the effect is that there is a seemingly unending variety in the ways in which students choose to rate themselves on statements that, by the statistical analyses reported previously, are supposedly reasonably coherent scales. In effect, each statement is a scale in its own right, and it shares meaning with other statements only to a partial extent (i.e., the extent indicated by the statement-scale correlations discussed earlier).

In view of the wide variation in the way individual students rated themselves on the various statements of a scale, it was finally decided to use the median (middle) rating as a score for a person on a scale. In practice, the computed median was rounded to the nearest whole scale number except when the median fell exactly halfway between two whole numbers. These scores ended in .5. Both students in the illustration above scored medians of 5.0.

Inspection of the frequencies with which medians occurred at each of the seven points along each scale, in each of the 12 subgroups in each school system suggests that instead of the great variations in frequency distributions found for single statements, there is a very general tendency for the distributions of medians to have a high point which is not at the extreme at either end, but somewhere between, with lesser frequencies on either side. This was not true in every case, but nevertheless the median seemed to be the most promising way of indicating where a student placed himself on any scale. Once the decision to use the median was reached, it was thereafter treated statistically just as though it were a score from a conventional test having right and wrong answers.

A question about the adequacy of this logic may well arise if you note that first I speak of simple tabulations of frequencies in which the responses of any group tend to pile up to a greater or lesser degree at the extremes of an attitude scale, and second I speak of a measure (individual medians of ratings of statements in a scale) which is not often distributed in a severely asymmetrical way. Remembering the responses of the illustrative students reported earlier, I think it clear that the variety of statements in a scale is great enough to make the median essentially a reflection of how many statements an individual chooses to rate as true or untrue of him. It is still possible, but according to the evidence rather unlikely, for a person to put nearly all his ratings at +3 or −3; more probable is his balancing out nearer midscale. Variations in the latter position have the consequence of producing a considerably more symmetrical frequency distribution than is seen in the untreated data, as shown by actual computation of the frequencies at each point on each scale for each subgroup in the study (not given here). The median, used as an individual's score on a scale, is thus a particular consequence of particular procedures. In effect, the computational procedures give it meaning and limit its meaning, and this should not be forgotten.

There arises, in connection with the use of any instrument of measurement, the question of just how reliable are the scores one obtains with it. There are frequently used procedures for calculating or estimating the reliability of tests or other measuring instruments when the questions can be scored as right or wrong, or yes-no. Unfortunately, however, the reliability of scales like the ones described here is not so easy to determine. After debate and consultation it was decided that the only feasible method was a very familiar one: divide any scale randomly in half (e.g., odd-numbered and even-numbered statements), and for each student find a median for each half, then correlate the medians for a group. By what is known as the Spearman-Brown Prophecy Formula one can then estimate the probable reliability of the full length of scale.

Four points should be understood about the data to be reported below. The first is that anonymously answered questionnaires are not noted for high reliability because of all the unknown possibilities for inconsistency in the responses. The second is that the restricted-range problem remains with us. The third is that, especially when a scale contains as few as 11 statements, one of the medians for any student is derived from only 5 statements and the other from 6. Reliabilities estimated in such a manner are not likely to be impressively large because the subsamples of statements on which they are based are so small and chance could so readily affect the results. The fourth point is that in line with the general attempt to keep analyses at the level of all the subgroups, all reliability computations were based on the 12 subgroups within each school system. But to arrive at a single correlation coefficient portraying the reliability of a scale, the 12 coefficients were averaged for Schools A, B, and C into a mean coefficient for each system and finally into a "grand mean" for all three schools combined (see table 1). Just how different the result would have been had all the students been combined for just a single calculation cannot be guessed, but the present method allows anyone interested in any datum in the following results sections (e.g., the mean score for any subgroup in a particular school) to go directly to appendix C and find out how reliably the scale he is interested in functioned in that group.

It will readily be apparent to anyone who has dealt with tests and measurements that it would have been more satisfactory had the reliabilities of the scales been higher, especially for the two short scales concerning liking for teachers and social distractibility. Just how large the coefficient should be is, of course, a matter of judgment depending upon the conditions under which measure-

Table 1. Reliability Coefficients for Specific Scales and Schools

Scale	School	Range of Spearman-Brown correlations	Mean correlation	Grand mean
Positive and	A	.59-.83	.74	
active	B	.58-.87	.76	
liking	C	.61-.81	.69	.73
Generalized	A	.54-.74	.68	
dislike	B	.56-.78	.67	
	C	.40-.80	.66	.67
Conscientious-	A	.56-.81	.73	
ness	B	.53-.84	.70	
	C	.58-.84	.74	.72
Anxiety-guilt	A	.55-.80	.67	
	B	.52-.76	.66	
	C	.27-.76	.66	.66
Liking for	A	.31-.70	.56	
teachers	B	.39-.75	.57	
	C	.41-.66	.56	.56
Social dis-	A	.43-.80	.58	
tractibility	B	.36-.77	.58	
	C	.45-.85	.58	.58
Orientation	A	.50-.79	.67	
toward future	B	.45-.76	.64	
	C	.51-.83	.69	.67

ments are made and for what purpose. Here the only intent is to compare rather large groups of students, and it will turn out that the scales with lowest reliabilities will be found to provide us with sensible information, even though we know that with more satisfactory reliabilities such information would be more exact and perhaps more sensible as a result. Considering that the response expected of students was an anonymous judgment concerning a personal reaction and the intensity of it, we can hardly expect the precision of measurement that can be produced in a highly controlled laboratory situation with more exactly defined criteria for judgment.

Problems in Collecting Data

When data are gathered as they were in this study, as in many other "field" situations, one does not have full control over the operation; for example, one cannot be sure how any particular student reacted to being asked to fill out the questionnaire. There are a number of possible difficulties in deciding whether certain questionnaires must be rejected from the research. Some of these difficulties are behavioral, some clerical, some nuisances, and at least one in the present studies was an amusing nuisance.

Even though emphasis is placed on anonymity, a rare student in the upper grades of Schools A, B, and C felt that he had been beat upon by tests and questions just once too often, so he deliberately set about making his paper useless. He might circle the same number for every statement on a page, omit a whole page of statements but draw a line across it, make his circled numbers into some kind of design which was visible and nonsensical, and write obscenities on the questionnaire. It is impossible to be sure every one of these occurrences has been spotted and the paper discarded, but it would appear that the person who thus psychologically thumbs his nose at the questionnaire (or its maker) wants to be sure that this action is not wasted, so that in one way or another he makes it easily detected. Careful attention to answer patterns and to student editing of statements, etc., seemed to uncover some such papers, and one can only hope that since the total number of papers was rather large, if one or more has been missed it will have had little effect on the final results. (The aggressive response is almost totally by males. The rare girls who were unhappy about the task usually started it and then simply stopped.)

A kind of clerical problem, apparently, is that of the omitted answer. We found that in a very large number of papers there would be a small proportion with several answers omitted. Any paper from which more than three answers were omitted was discarded; fortunately, computer programs can be written which allow for missing data, so that if one student in 130 did not respond to a particular statement, that fact was duly allowed for in the computations. My interpretation of this particular kind of problem is that conscientious students pass over statements on which they are not ready to make a quick judgment, and in going back to answer later fail to remedy certain omissions.

Another essentially clerical problem resulted when entire home-rooms failed to fill in the first line on the cover page of questions; as previously mentioned, grade, sex, etc., were to be indicated on that line. Since the lack of classificatory information made these papers useless, the problem was more serious. I can only speculate that the teacher who had read my suggestions for administering the questionnaire had misunderstood my request and told the class to omit that line. The omissions occurred either in a whole class or almost not at all, and then as seemingly random happenings.

Finally—and fortunately I had some forewarning of this problem in preliminary data collection—there was the matter of discovering accurately the sex of the respondent. Innocently enough, in the first run I had simply included in the first line a space for: Sex___, in the expectation that *M* or *F* would be the reply. Instead, the answer was frequently "As often as possible" or "I'm too young" or "My parents don't approve" or other ingenious responses, which of course wasted all the rest of the student's work because without sex identification the paper had to be discarded. In the next try, I asked for: Sex (M___ or F___). A fairly sizeable number of students chose not to put an *X* or a checkmark in one of the spaces and instead carefully blocked out the *M* or the *F*, and of course it was not clear whether the blocking out indicated the correct or the incorrect answer. There were a few students who could not resist the temptation to give both answers, which didn't help either. The final version is adequate, so far as I know. I simply indicated, on two lines:

Circle correct one
Male   Female

and apart from the possibility that the incorrect answer may have been given deliberately, there were very few visible indications of ambiguity or fun and games; the latter usually took the form of an empty oval between the two labels. It should be remembered that all papers from which classificatory information was missing were discarded. In Schools A, B, and C, I believe, this introduced no important sampling bias.

The Schools and Their Communities

As was indicated in the very early description of the purposes of this research, one factor that plays a part in the results of many social-science investigations is the socioeconomic level of individuals or groups involved. Similarly it was thought here that the socioeconomic level of the community in which the school system existed might be reflected in what I earlier referred to as the "quality of the school" (by way of parental education and expectations, talent and interests of peers, resources available to schools, and so on). Socioeconomic status, however, is both complex and difficult to define and does not necessarily determine the quality of schools. (For example, suppose that in a suburb there lived a large number of wealthy people who all sent their children away to private schools; they probably would be unwilling to pay high taxes to support an excellent school system for the less wealthy families in the town.)

In my original plan to request permission to collect data in different school systems, I felt it would be impolitic to emphasize my interest in comparing systems existing in socioeconomically different communities, for I simply did not know whether any sensitivities would be offended by such an interest. As it turned out, my concern was unfounded, but what I in fact did initially in deciding where to apply was to talk to teachers and administrators whom I knew, in towns in which I knew I would not wish to carry on my research. That talk was largely in terms of professional opinions about the quality of school systems and amateur opinions about the quality of communities. Later I discovered that the systems in which I worked not only cheerfully supplied me with fact sheets about their schools with occasional commentary about the community, but responded promptly and cooperatively when I wrote to ask questions beyond those answered by the fact sheet. So let me give a brief description of the three communities and school systems which are of central interest here. The actual facts given are not in the same categories for all towns, for I preferred, with some exceptions, to take the information provided and to avoid "pushiness" in this matter. Information about each high school had been assembled for use by college admissions officers and other interested persons. Assuming that junior high schools resemble the high schools to which most of their graduates go, I shall speak here as though I have data on the whole system, which, of course, I do not.

School A is described in its fact sheet as being in a socioeconomically lower- to middle-class community. It is a suburb of a medium-sized city, and most of its residents are said to work there in business offices, retail outlets, or factories. There is also, I learned from other sources, a substantial manual-labor group, and there are relatively few professional families. The fact sheet describes the high school as comprehensive, with a flexible curriculum including general, business, and college preparatory programs. For college-bound students there are special classes in English, mathematics, biology, and English history. Among more than 100 seniors who elected to take the December 1968 Scholastic Aptitude Tests, the mean verbal score was 456. (These Tests are so standardized that the nation-wide average of students choosing to take them is 500.) The mean mathematics score was 492. Colleges being attended by graduates are listed in the fact sheet without an indication as to how many graduates attend a particular institution. There seem to be three justifiable remarks to make about the list. First, the colleges vary from two generally regarded as among the best in the country to institutions much less famous. Second, a number of the institutions are junior, community, or technical colleges. Third, at the risk of being offensive, I would guess that a good many of the institutions are ones which many college faculty members regard as lower-echelon in quality. Apart from the college preparatory classes mentioned above, an official of the system (not the principal) informed me that there are few special programs in the system. The same person believed that most of the newer teachers in the system were prepared for teaching in our various state colleges (which not long ago were single-purpose, i.e., teacher-training, colleges) or in the school of education at the state university. Both student and teacher annual turnover were believed to be low. One final remark about the community: there has been considerable public dispute about financial problems in the governance of the town, and since schools tend to be a very costly portion of a town budget, one can readily infer that administration and teacher salaries and school resources are closely eyed; it would not be unreasonable to expect low morale or other problems among faculty and staff.

School B is described in its fact sheet as a suburb of the same medium-sized city referred to above. An official of the system reports that the population of the community is rather heterogeneous from a socioeconomic point of view, since it contains laboring, clerical, and sales personnel, many of whom work in the nearby city, and relatively numerous professional people, most of whom also work in the city. The high school curriculum has several levels and several tracks; in addition the fact sheet lists four characteristics of the school: the use of the audiolingual approach in foreign languages, the use of composition critics, the offering of advanced chemistry and biology, and a provision for independent studies. An advanced-placement program is offered in English. For students graduating in 1969 the average verbal score on the Scholastic Aptitude Test (presumably taken in December 1968) was 493 and the average mathematics score was 516. In relation to the following remarks about college attendance, it may be worth noting that although School B is only a little more than half the size of School A, nearly as many students in the former elected to take the Scholastic Aptitude Tests. According to the fact sheet 49 percent of the class were admitted to four-year colleges, 15 percent to two-year colleges and 9 percent to technical colleges, business schools, and other vocational training institutions. There is no indication as to which colleges were attended. An administrator indicated that there are several special educational programs and a variety of education-related clubs. This person was also of the opinion that most newer teachers in the system were prepared for teaching in liberal arts institutions with teacher-preparation departments or programs. The same source said there was a low annual turnover rate of students and an "average" turnover rate for teachers. From the fact that a sizable number of professional families choose to live in the town and send their offspring to the local schools, one may infer that the system is at least adequate, if not somewhat better, from their point of view.

While some doubt may remain as to just exactly where to place School B, there is little doubt about School C. Its fact sheet describes the community as having a high socioeconomic level. It too is a suburb, but of a different medium-sized city, and many of its citizens are employed there, particularly in managerial and executive positions in large businesses and other kinds of operations. The description of the available educational offerings in the high school handbook is impressive indeed: in the humanities area a student may, if qualified, take a course correlating literature, history, music, and art; or creative writing; or dramatics; or any of five languages. There is advanced-placement (college-level) English, French, and Spanish; a wide variety of mathematics courses at quite advanced levels, including four in addition to the two advanced-placement courses. Biology is also represented at ordinary and advanced-placement levels, and the same is true of chemistry and physics. A total of ten history courses is offered, with the two for advanced placement covering modern European history and United States history. In addition, there are many offerings in business education and industrial arts, as well as home economics, art, and music.

Of the class of 1969, 86 percent had elected to take the Scholastic Aptitude Tests; their mean verbal score was 502 and their mean mathematics score 532. The class produced 14 National Merit Finalists and 49 of its members received letters of commendation. (The figures for the class of 1969 include students from the other high school in the same suburb. All other figures cited here are for the one high school in which data were collected for this research.) The list of colleges the graduates attended is long and, in the four-year group, includes just about every prestigious institution in the country, as well as a rather large number of what might fairly be called top-echelon institutions.

It is clear that the schools in this system have a rich offering for their students; their programs include a lecture series, college professors in residence each year to assist students doing independent work in some area, a visiting-artist program, student-exchange programs with an inner-city high school, and student tours and visits. In fact, in the Principal's Annual Report to the parents for the year 1968-69, he found it desirable to remark on more than 40 different features of the school's program or year, and many of these sound interesting and innovative indeed. Information concerning the background of teachers and either student or teacher turnover was not sought, but it is easy to believe this school system would retain its students and that good teachers would gravitate toward it.

The three town and school populations are similar in that they are suburban and contain very few nonwhite families. That Schools A and C are poles apart, at least in terms of "inputs" to the educational process (and in one specific instance of "outputs," namely, the number of college entrances and quality of colleges entered) seems to be established. That School B is somewhere between is very probable, but a flat statement about the exact degree of its similarity or dissimilarity to the other systems seems unwise. It was disturbing at first to note that there was, in Schools A and B particularly, considerable variability in the sizes of the 12 subgroups, especially in the higher grades. My first reaction was that this might reflect the number of dropouts, but as I have indicated earlier this is probably not involved. Rather, three other factors may be implicated. First, there was variation in the timing of in-migration surges. A second factor has been referred to before, namely, that I have no way of knowing exactly which groups are missing whole homerooms of papers because classificatory information was omitted by all members of one or more classes (which might even have been from the same grade). And third, in a period of expanding enrollments and construction of buildings or other facilities, the school systems were forced to locate students physically according to the immediate realities, so that I may have missed certain students who happened to be located elsewhere.

7. INTENSITY AND DIRECTION OF ATTITUDES TOWARD SCHOOL

It will be remembered that each of the seven scales measuring attitude components contains exactly the same set of statements, as the scales were used in Schools A, B, and C. It therefore seems appropriate to focus this discussion on one scale at a time. This permits us, incidentally, to comment on similarities and differences among the schools, having in the back of our minds the fact that they supposedly differ in "quality." The most easily understood presentation seems to be afforded by graphs showing average scores in each of the 12 subgroups in the three school systems. For exact data consult the appropriate part of appendix D; I shall refer to comparisons of schools by way of analyses shown as the last entries in each part of appendix D.

The statistical procedure used in making various comparisons is known as the analysis of variance. No attempt will be made here to explicate this kind of analysis, but it is perhaps useful to indicate one result of it which a reader of any graph may utilize. In the body of the graph may be found an entry such as sex = <.001. It is sufficient for our purposes to realize that this "level of significance" is to be read as follows: if the true variation between the self-ratings of the two sexes were in fact zero (this is called the null hypothesis), a large number of replications of the observations symbolized by the means in a particular graph would yield *by chance alone* fewer than 1 in 1000 differences between means for the sexes as large as the difference being inspected at the particular moment. The "leap of faith" is then taken by the investigator, as though he said to himself, *this* isn't that one chance occasion, and so he concludes that the null hypothesis (no difference) should be rejected. Various levels of significance (.05, .01, .001, or other) may be chosen in advance as prerequisite before the investigator will judge that the null hypothesis should be rejected, and this judgment is influenced by a good many factors which will not be discussed. It should be mentioned, however, that since the number of individuals in most of the comparisons reported here is relatively large, a small difference can look very significant when in fact it is of no real importance in the judgment of the investigator or the reader. It will be remembered that I remarked earlier on the deliberate use of the 12 subgroups in any school system as a (rather artificial) device to ensure that very large numbers of observations did not lead to overconfident evaluations of correlation coefficients. Exactly the same conservatism is now to govern the reporting of analyses of variance: a fairly demanding criterion of significance, ordinarily the .01 level, will be used as the basis for evaluating the outcomes of any analysis of variance. (This is not lightly decided; if one uses too demanding a criterion of significance, he may reject the null hypothesis in error.)

One additional kind of entry will be found in the body of each graph. It reads S x G (S *by* G) and is called an interaction term. It means, very simply, that one is testing to see whether one main variable (e.g., sex) interacts with the other in such a way that whether a difference between sexes is significant depends upon which grade one is talking about; or the reverse statement may be made—that a significant variation across grades depends upon which sex one is talking about. The interaction term is evaluated according to the level of significance it reaches, exactly as are the main effects discussed in the preceding paragraph.

Another remark about the graphs should be made, for it reflects an arbitrary solution to a question about how to present the data. The vertical axis always runs in the direction of "more of the attitude" being pictured in the graph. For example, the higher a point is on a graph showing liking for school, the stronger the degree of liking. It is a little more difficult to remember, when looking at a graph showing degree of generalized dislike for school, that the numbers run exactly the same way. That is, a high mean on the vertical axis would point to great dislike for school. (The reason for my choosing this particular example will become clear shortly.)

Scale 1: Positive and Active Liking for School

Exhibited in figure 1 are the curves depicting average or mean

Figure 1
Mean Degree of Positive and Active Liking

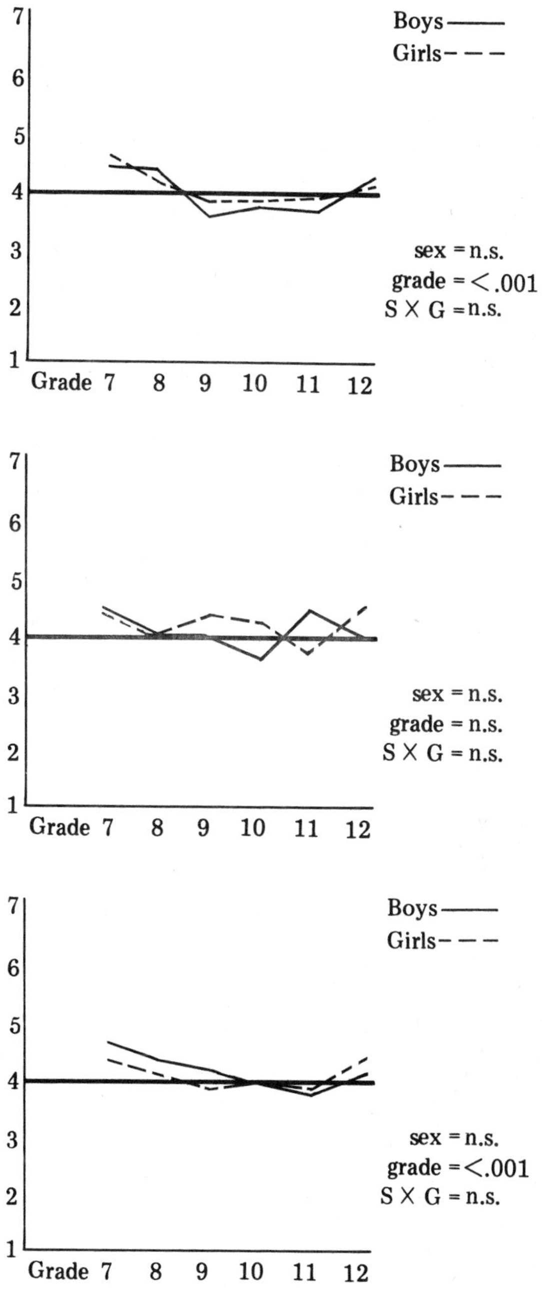

School A

School B

School C

strength of liking in Schools A, B, and C. The scale itself is to be
found in appendix B.

Perhaps the most obvious thing about these curves for School
A is that they depart very little from 4.0, which you will remember is defined as "in between" or "don't know." In the main,
then, except for one significant variation to be mentioned in a
moment, the prevailing attitude in School A as measured by this
scale is indifference, apathy, or something akin to this. The difference between the sexes is totally insignificant statistically, but
the variations across the grades are quite significant even though
not impressively large. Examination of the curves suggests that
this comes about because, in both sexes, there appears to be
some (small) average liking for school in the earlier and later
grades, but something less than neutrality in the middle grades.
Since both sexes show about the same general trend, the S x G
interaction is totally insignificant.

The meaning of the finding of general apathy is debatable. A
classic reaction to the notion that the average student is indifferent to school is that, after all, "kids are expected to talk that
way." But in this study, if anyone had really wished to depart
from what "kids are expected to say" he could have done so without any of his peers or anyone else being aware of it. I am inclined
to take the average results as probably valid, and to go on to two
other statements which may be elaborations of the obvious. The
first is, despite the tone of, say, some of Friedenberg's or Keniston's writings, there must be a fairly large number of students
who are *not* alienated from school, and they are to be found in
the upper part of each distribution of scores around a mean. It
is equally true that in the lower part of each distribution must
fall students who indeed have little liking for school, who probably could be called alienated from it. So on the dimension
measured here, there are all kinds of students and it is clear
there are a good many willing to say they like school. It does
concern me, as it must any reader, that the averages are depress-
ingly close to indifference and that, therefore, many students
by definition have to be at or near this point. Incidentally, for
those who believe that girls like school better than boys, this
particular scale hardly shows it.

Concerning the curves for School B, it can only be said that they reveal nothing new; in fact, the only previously significant variation in School A, that across grades, disappears here. There is simply no significant variation for sex or grade or the interaction of the two. But we do find the same tendency toward apathy on the average.

To pass on to School C, we discover the same picture as for School A: only the variation across grades is significant, and in it the pattern is roughly the same, with the lower grades and the seniors showing somewhat inconsistently higher average degrees of liking for school.

The empirical findings, then, are quite clear. The sexes, at all grade levels, react to school in about the same way. As to grade variations, we might note that on the whole the trend in junior high school (grades 7, 8, and 9 in Schools A and C; grades 7 and 8 in School B) is downward, then in senior high school, rather uncertainly and with several exceptions, upward. Although the significance level of the grade variations is high, this is one of those instances in which one has a hard time making himself believe the variation across grades is of great importance.

It is worth remarking (or, probably, debating) that if attitude toward school (in this case, positive and active liking) is considered an output of schooling, the range of communities included here does not produce any variation, perhaps because the range is restricted compared to Coleman's very wide range (see 1968, p. 20); or because, as he elsewhere indicates (1966, p. 22), variation among white students' life circumstances does not seem to be as important as among other groups; or because attitudes as here measured in grades 7 through 12 are a very different kind of indicator than any he used. It is hard for me to believe, however, that the differences between community and school in A and in C are not great, yet that difference is not related to attitude whether it is regarded as output *or* input. Although the analysis is not shown here (see pp. 140-46), a comparison of the three schools on this scale shows that the variation across grades is highly significant statistically. In view of the fact that it does not reach significance in School B, and the variations in the other two schools are not large even though in each case they are significant, it would seem reasonable to suppose that when the schools are combined in the comparison, the sheer weight of numbers of students is more of a factor in the significant grade variation than is the level of liking for school they express. This must be qualified by a reminder that only suburban schools are considered here. But I should emphasize that the typical school system, administrator, or teacher is likely to have all degrees of liking to cope with, and the large group of students near the mean is simply in school without liking it.

Scale 2: Generalized Dislike of School

In view of the fact that the scale purporting to measure positive and active liking for school on the average showed no such thing, it would seem unnecessary to use other scales having to do with any aspect of this general attitude. Preliminary work persistently seemed to indicate, however, that there is at least one subtlety about the failure of students to declare, on the average, very much liking for school. This persistence was exhibited in recurrent suggestive findings that there is a group of statements to which students react in a way that is different from the way they react to statements about liking school, and this may indicate something about both adolescent personality and reactions to school. Scale 2 (see appendix B), with its rather arbitrary label, was constructed, and the outcomes of its use are portrayed in figure 2.

In rather striking contrast to what might be inferred from the curves for School A on scale 1, it is clear here that on the average the students *deny disliking school.* On this scale, in contrast also to the first one, there is a highly significant sex difference, for girls more strongly deny disliking school than do boys. There is also a highly significant but perhaps less impressive variation across the grades, with those in the upper grades denying more strongly that they dislike school than those in the lower grades. (This is consistent with the suggestive but small increase in liking for school shown by scale 1.) The interaction between the two main effects is wholly insignificant.

There may be some effect here of what is called "response set." That is, if one looks closely at the statements contained in scale 2, there is the possibility that wittingly or unwittingly a student might not wish to agree that certain statements are very true of

Figure 2
Mean Degree
of Generalized Dislike

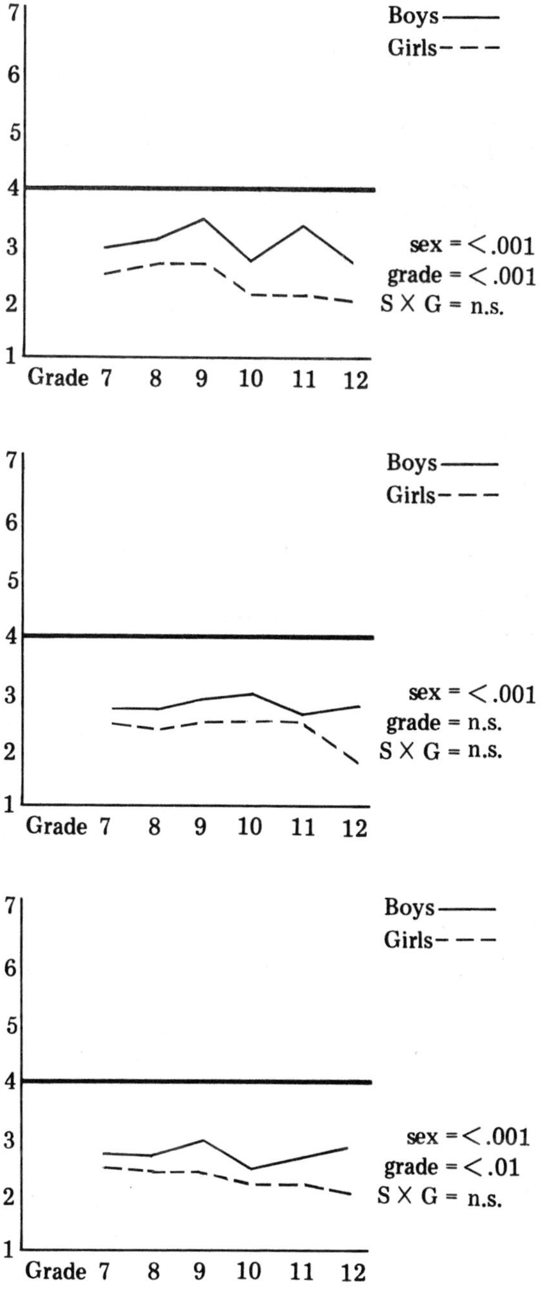

School A

School B

School C

him or even partly true, for they are in a sense derogatory. The extent to which this influenced responses when the student was anonymous cannot be evaluated, but it should be recognized that the means shown for scale 2 are perhaps low. However, they would have to be greatly increased before they would remove the impression of a paradox, or more exactly a dilemma: on the average, students do not admit to liking school, but on the average they rather definitely refuse to admit to disliking it. They evidently are just there, and one can guess that many are in conflict about it. It is also just possible that the students in fact are being truthful—they are so apathetic toward school that it would be incorrect for them to say they disliked it.

The findings for School B are similar to those for School A but somewhat more extreme (in 9 of the 12 subgroup comparisons that can be made with School A). Again the sexes differ at a high level of significance, with girls denying more strongly that they dislike school. This time, however, the variation across grades does not reach a satisfactory enough level of significance for us to take it seriously, and there is no interaction between the two main effects. The remarks made about the seemingly paradoxical refusal to admit disliking school, in School A, apply equally here, however.

If we look now at the findings for School C, we see a third and slightly more extreme instance of the denial of disliking school. Here the sex difference is in the same direction as in the other schools, and highly significant. Since even the boys, in the main, are fairly close to the bottom of the scale, a difference between the sexes is possible only because there is such low variability of individuals within each group about their mean; the most extreme example is the twelfth-grade girls, approximately two-thirds of whom, as indicated in appendix D by the standard deviations, rate themselves within one step from the end of the scale. The variation across grades is significant but not extremely so, and the interaction between sex and grade is of no significance whatever.

This scale, then, shows a significant tendency for what I have called the higher quality school system in the more affluent community to produce the strongest mean denial of dislike for school, especially among girls; the presumably intermediate-quality school was next in this respect. Grade variations across the schools are statistically very significant, but again they do not seem important. The meaning of this denial continues to be somehow paradoxical: the students have refused, on the average, to rate themselves as liking school (scale 1) and now, instead of taking that same neutral position on scale 2 rather firmly rate themselves, on the average, as denying they have *this* attitude. Perhaps there is no better place for them to spend time during school hours, at least no other place where one's friends are to be found. (The possibility of "response set" remains, although I do not take it as quantitatively very important. Consider that an individual's score on the scale was merely his middle rating among the statements on it; several of his ratings could be affected somewhat without necessarily changing his median.) And there is always the possibility that the students are telling the truth.

Scale 3: Conscientiousness

From the beginning of these studies it was clear that a group of statements clustered together around the theme of conscientiousness about schoolwork. Along with scale 4, to be presented in the next section, this scale was easiest to construct, in the sense that the clearcut clustering of statements gave confidence that there indeed was some dimension of attitude toward school which could be measured. The statements used are included in appendix B, and the results secured with the scale are shown in figure 3.

In School A two results come out at a high level of significance: as in the stereotype, girls are more conscientious than boys, on the average, but there is a gradual lessening of conscientiousness as the students pass upward through the school (and, we assume, progress through adolescence). The interaction between these two main effects is entirely insignificant, i.e., the difference between the sexes is rather similar at all grade levels, and the changes across the grades are approximately the same for boys and for girls.

Approximately the same results are obtained in School B, where again girls are more conscientious than boys, at a highly significant statistical level. It is also true that variations across the grades are statistically highly significant, apparently because both sexes show

Figure 3
Mean Degree of Conscientiousness

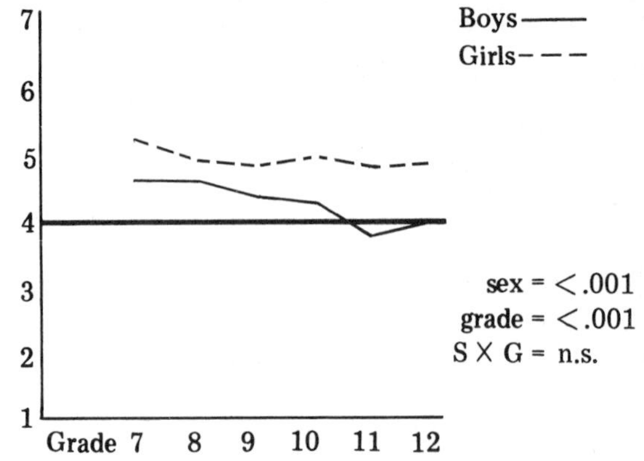
Boys
Girls
7
6
5
4
3
2
1
Grade 7 8 9 10 11 12
sex = <.001
grade = <.001
S X G = n.s.

School A

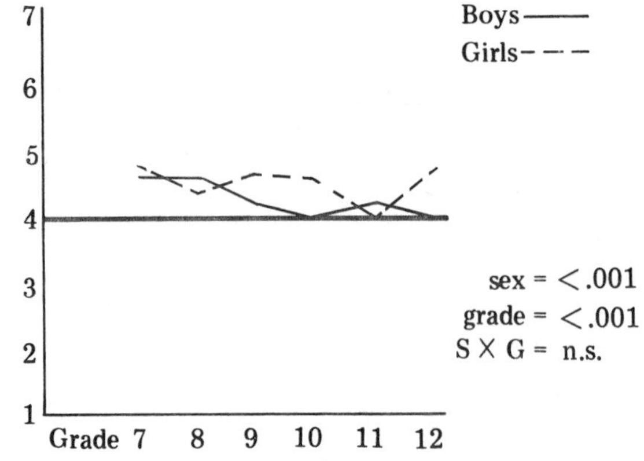
Boys
Girls
7
6
5
4
3
2
1
Grade 7 8 9 10 11 12
sex = <.001
grade = <.001
S X G = n.s.

School B

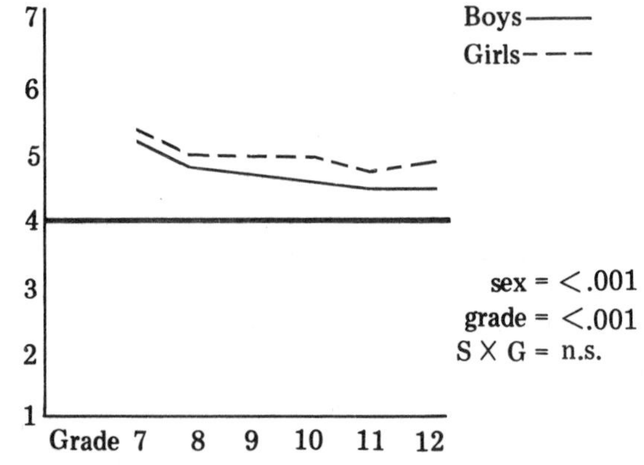
Boys
Girls
7
6
5
4
3
2
1
Grade 7 8 9 10 11 12
sex = <.001
grade = <.001
S X G = n.s.

School C

a general decline until there is a steep rise in senior year for the girls. The interaction between the two main factors of sex and grade is altogether insignificant.

In School C the findings are much the same. In general, the students here are more conscientious than elsewhere. Along with this observation, note that there is still a sex difference, with girls being more conscientious. There is also still a variation across the grades, with the more advanced students rating themselves as less conscientious. Both findings are statistically highly significant, and the variations are large enough to permit one to attach some importance to them. (The interaction between the two main effects was again entirely insignificant.)

Whether one regards conscientiousness of students as an input or an output of schooling (plus earlier influences), it is worthy of note here that what I have called the most favored school system contains students who given themselves higher ratings (see appendix D) on conscientiousness than students in other school systems. They did not give themselves higher ratings for liking school, and they tended to deny more strongly that they disliked school. As remarked at an earlier point, this makes for interesting speculation about child-rearing practices in community C. It seems quite reasonable to suppose that successful parents living in an affluent community would rear their children in such a way that the children would expect and be expected to do whatever they did to the best of their ability.

One does not necessarily have to like it, but if the activity or the accomplishment is expected, it will be done. I cannot help but feel that this sort of background may underlie not only the ratings students gave themselves on scale 3 in School C, but also behind the high performance of the top students in the graduating class there, which often led to admission into excellent colleges, and the level of competence indicated by the considerable number of National Merit semifinalist and finalist ratings. Be that as it may, the average response on scale 1 was apathy toward school, so that one begins to sense an essentially joyless, dutiful school experience. This probably is not true of those at the "top of the heap," for they succeed in and are rewarded for many things, even though, like my Yale students described earlier, they probably find much to complain of concerning school.

Only in this very speculative way can one say that the findings of scale 3 are in some degree in accord with Coleman's findings.

As appendix D shows, sex and grade vary quite significantly across schools, from a statistical point of view. Since these results occur in every statistical test at a high level of significance, I am inclined to believe them. An interesting aspect of the across-schools analysis is a significant interaction of schools and sexes. Inspection of the three main sub-tables in appendix D suggests that this interaction stems from the high ratings girls give themselves on conscientiousness in School A as compared to the boys there. The grand means for the groups in question, weighted according to the number of students contributing to each, are shown below.

	School A	*School B*	*School C*
Boys	4.3	4.4	4.6
Girls	4.9	4.7	5.0
Difference	.6	.3	.4

Scale 4: Anxiety and Guilt about School

There were several reasons for constructing and using this scale. The first was that Sarason (1960) and his colleagues had built a considerable conceptual and empirical background for expecting that anxiety in its various manifestations would be associated with school in many students, and one can easily expect it to interact with other attitudes toward school. The second was that in the previously reported preliminary work, which led me to change strategy and to construct scales to measure attitudes, there persistently occurred a cluster of statements (several of them edited forms of Sarason's questions, others from various sources) which related to each other fairly well but not at all closely or consistently to other kinds of statements. The third might be called common sense: any parent or school-person knows that student tension and concern can be associated with aspects of school, sometimes many aspects of school. It therefore seemed highly desirable to assess it in the students studied here and to determine its relation to the other aspects of attitude measured. As earlier remarked, the scale was relatively easy to assemble (see appendix B) because of the way the statements in it correlated with one another during the so-called item-analysis phase. Results for scale 4 are depicted in figure 4.

Figure 4
Mean Degree of Anxiety-Guilt

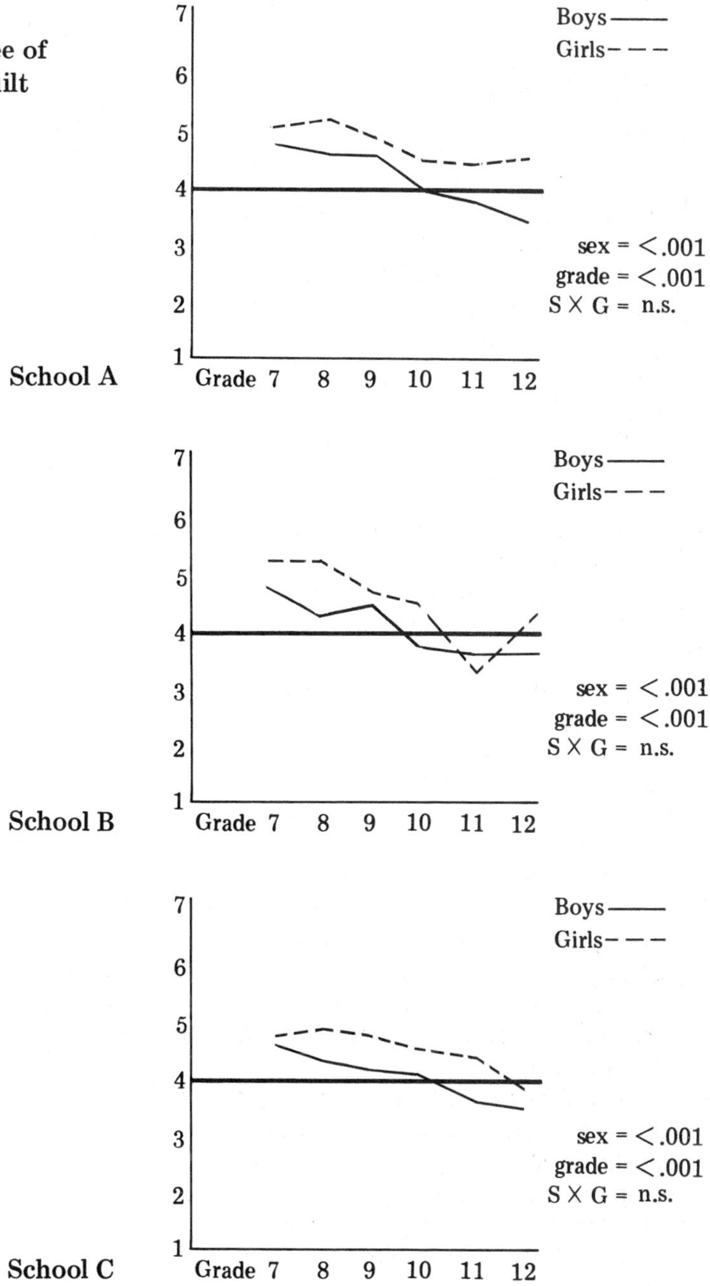
School A
7
6
5
4
3
2
1
Grade 7 8 9 10 11 12
Boys ——
Girls - - -
sex = <.001
grade = <.001
S × G = n.s.
School B
7
6
5
4
3
2
1
Grade 7 8 9 10 11 12
Boys ——
Girls - - -
sex = <.001
grade = <.001
S × G = n.s.
School C
7
6
5
4
3
2
1
Grade 7 8 9 10 11 12
Boys ——
Girls - - -
sex = <.001
grade = <.001
S × G = n.s.

We can readily see that in School A girls were very significantly more willing to rate themselves as having anxiety and guilt feelings about school than were the boys. Similarly, there was a very significant shift in the amount of anxiety indicated, for it decreased noticeably in the upper grades. This was true for both sexes, so the interaction term was totally insignificant. With Sarason's work in the background I am ready to take both main findings seriously.

We can see the same general picture in School B, with highly significant sex differences, similarly significant grade variations, and an insignificant interaction. The mean values for the two sexes grade by grade show little difference.

When we move to School C, we again find that sex differences are highly significant, and this time they are in general larger. Grade variations are highly significant, with some decrease for both sexes in the upper grades, and with no significant interaction between the two main variables.

Three comments seem relevant here. The first two relate these findings to the work of Sarason and his associates in various studies. Most of their studies were done with a simple questionnaire, any respondent to which was readily identified. Regardless of how much weight one attaches to the latter point, the anxiety scores of boys were lower than those of girls on the Test Anxiety Scale for Children. Although the authors were somewhat concerned that the questions used might have tapped more things important to boys, this seems less likely with the TASC than with their General Anxiety Scale. But the important point of their interpretation was that it is less permissible for boys to express anxiety than for girls, and that this sex-role difference is conveyed to the child from an early age. Indeed, this idea leads to the expectation that the older children get, the more likely they are to conform to both the expectations of others and self-expectations. The present study, then, is consistent with Sarason's views and data. Sarason (1960, p. 253) and his colleagues specifically reject any conclusion that one sex is literally more anxious than the other, on the grounds of having no suitable evidence for drawing a conclusion on this point.

Second, the reasonableness of their argument concerning an increasing tendency among boys to suppress signs of anxiety might lead one to expect that among students as old as those studied here, boys would not readily admit to anxiety (or, by analogy, guilt) about school. Yet under conditions of anonymity, seventh-, eighth-, and ninth-grade boys do admit to such attitudes. Girls remain less inhibited (assuming the just-mentioned theory is correct) until junior and senior year in School B, senior year in School C, and throughout senior year in School A. This may be considered an extension of Sarason's findings into older age groups, with a technique that permits those who wish to do so anonymously to indicate the degree of anxious or guilty concern they feel.

Third, the fact that in all three schools girls show a steady downward trend is, so far as I know, a new finding in the anxiety area. There would appear to be several possible explanations, and there may be more or less truth in each of them. First, in these age groups sex-role learning may begin to include the notion of self-control or less inhibited expression, at least to a degree, for girls as well as for boys. Second, peer groups may be the source of, or the teacher of, such lessened expression. And third, the sheer process of maturation plus experience may result, in school, in lessened responsiveness to what were formerly worrisome situations.

The third comment above on the anxiety-guilt findings is in a way an expression of surprise. In two of the school systems in which I had done preliminary work, a high degree of anxiety and guilt was expressed in ratings of single statements. Conversations with school psychologists and directors of guidance indicated that they found this to be one of the most frequent problems confronting them in dealing with students. They felt this to be an expected circumstance in these two very wealthy, success-oriented towns where, in the opinion of the psychologists, parents put heavy pressure on children to do well in school, as a prelude to being successful in college and after college. (In both systems about 90 percent of the graduates went on to four-year colleges.)

School C in the present main study is in a community seemingly of much the same kind. But the students here, on the average, seem to show somewhat less anxiety and guilt than the students in Schools A and B. This comment cannot be extended at this time for two reasons: in the preliminary work I was not using

scales of the kind used here, and the change in method may have
caused a different impression; and before this main study I had
not gathered data in schools similar to the present A and B, so
that I may have been led to an erroneous impression of differences among communities and their children with respect to
anxiety and guilt. Yet the speculative possibilities remain that
inhibition training was stronger in C than in the communities
A and B, or self-confidence was greater.

The across-schools comparisons (appendix D) show that the
schools variation just barely reached significance, and variations
between pairs of schools do not seem impressive. Sex differences
and grade variations both yielded highly significant results. These
are probably to be taken seriously, for in all three schools the
girls clearly express more anxiety and guilt, and in all six subgroups (grades) there is a downward trend in the amount of anxiety and guilt shown in the self-ratings for each sex. There were
no significant interactions, and we are led to place heaviest weight
on the sex and the grade variations, and thereby on the socializa-
tion process in and out of school, as well as on sheer maturation.

Scale 5: Favorable Attitude toward Teachers

It would seem only reasonable that the attitude of a student
toward teachers would relate to his willingness to carry on schoolwork, the pleasure he gets from school, and so on. (Note that no
causality is implied by that sentence.) But there is a reasonably
widespread stereotype that students dislike teachers, because
they, like parents, are authority figures. It may just be the thing
to say, but in any case, as far as adults can tell, there is likely to
be more complaint about grouchy Miss So-and-So or unfair
Mr. Such-and-Such than there is praise for the well-liked teacher,
or the one perceived as expert or generous or whatever that person's outstanding traits may be. Hence, scale 5 (see appendix B)
was constructed—largely out of my head and remembered conversations as well as overheard ones. It turned out that my head
was a slightly less good source than the leads I had been able to
follow previously (only 11 of the 14 statements survived the item
analysis of the scale), but the results were consistent and are
shown in figure 5. (Remember that the grand mean of reliability
coefficients for this scale is the lowest in the study: .56.)

Figure 5
Mean Degree
of Liking for Teachers

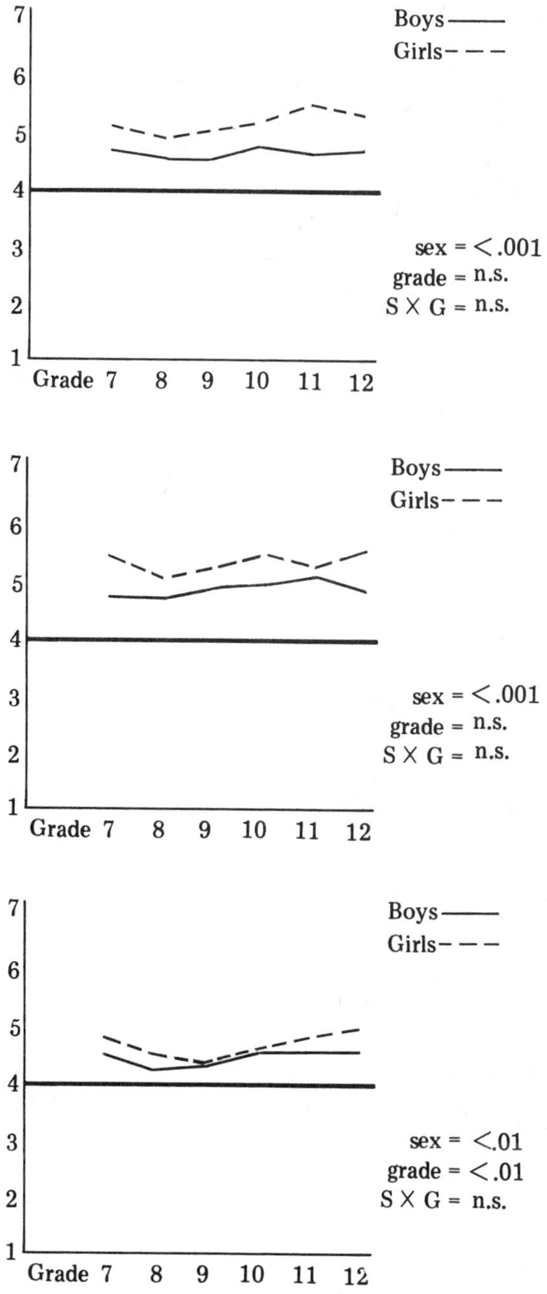

School A

sex = < .001
grade = n.s.
S × G = n.s.

School B

sex = < .001
grade = n.s.
S × G = n.s.

School C

sex = < .01
grade = < .01
S × G = n.s.

In School A, perhaps the first thing that strikes the eye (at least mine) is that the students, in general, tend to *like* teachers, the girls very significantly more than the boys, with means sufficiently different to be worth taking seriously. The variation across grades does not quite reach significance and is without a clear trend in either sex. The interaction is, of course, insignificant.

When we look at School B, we again see just about the same thing: a very significant sex difference, the girls being more favorable at every grade level. In this school, however, the variation across grades is so inconsistent that the result is statistically without significance, as is true of the interaction.

School C, in comparison with the other two schools, presents a rather mixed effect. The girls still like teachers better than do boys, and the result is significant but at a lower level than in the other schools. The grade variation is for the first time significant but at the same level as the sex difference; the interaction is not significant, so that we must cancel out one possible explanation of the grade variations suggested by the graph, namely, that there appears to be a more systematic decrease, then increase, in liking for teachers among the girls than among the boys. The grade variation, as far as I can judge, has to be regarded as rather unimpressive despite what the significance test says.

One aspect of the findings in School C is interesting as a stimulus to speculation. The fact is that with one exception (eleventh-grade boys in School A), the average liking for teachers is lower at every grade level in School C than in the other two schools (even the exception is a tie). Why should the students in the more favored setting, which in all likelihood attracts high-quality teachers (define the term quality broadly for present purposes) appear to like teachers less? One guess is that in such a community there are many significant adults, and against such a backdrop, teachers are relatively not as outstanding as available adults whose example and friendship can be valued and respected. Whether this is a real or imaginary state of affairs, it is still true in School C that teachers are in general liked.

What remains unevaluated is the probability that, in contrast with grade school, the junior and senior high school faculties include a much higher proportion of male teachers. This must surely create a new set of conditions as far as attitude toward teachers is concerned, especially for the older students, and the conditions could have quite different meanings for the two sexes. The across-school comparison (appendix D) shows that the schools differ at a high level of significance. This is probably to be taken seriously, for in School C all six grade-levels of girls rate themselves as liking teachers less than the girls in the other two schools, and with the exception of one tie in twelve comparisons, the same is true of the boys, to a lesser degree. Such consistency probably means that we have again found School C to be different, but not necessarily in a way likely to be related to better performance.

The sex and grade comparisons are highly reliable, as the previously reported results for individual schools would lead one to expect. But there is an additional finding: a significant interaction between school and sex. As shown in the small table following the (weighted) grand means for the sexes do seem to depend upon which school we are talking about. The sex difference in School C is noticeably smaller than in the other two schools, which is what was said above.

	School A	*School B*	*School C*
Boys	4.6	4.7	4.5
Girls	5.1	5.3	4.7
Difference	−.5	−.6	−.2

Scale 6: Social Distractibility

This scale was suggested by an early study on achievement motivation by Applezweig et al. (1956). Their research indicated that academic achievement by a particular student was related not only to that student's strength of need to achieve well, but to the typical performance of the student's friends. From this it is but a short step to the idea that the peer groups to which we attach such importance among adolescents are as likely to influence attitudes toward school as they are to influence any other aspect of the behavior of a group member. However, it is not readily apparent what that influence might be, for a particular peer group might support the idea of excellence in school, have little interest in school, or discourage the idea of excellence in schoolwork.

Since time spent with friends in school seems most likely to be a break from academic routine, I decided to define the variable to be measured simply as social distractibility. This does not so much imply an attitude toward school as, perhaps, toward other students, but the implication is that the greater the concern about friends or friendships, the less is the concern about school. This, it should be remembered is here an assumption, not an empirical statement. (Support for it will be found in the next chapter.) As was true for the scale measuring attitude toward teachers, 3 of the 14 statements included in the presumptive scale did not survive item analysis, so this is a scale with fewer statements than might be desired (see appendix B).

When we look at the data for School A as pictured in figure 6 it becomes clear that there is, in general, not much distractibility (although all but one of the means are definitely above 4.0). But the apparently greater distractibility among girls is not really significant, and the variation across grades is quite random, so that neither it nor the interaction of the two main variables is significant. Almost exactly the same things may be said about School B, as seen in figure 6, except for a slight (not enough to be significant) appearance of denial of social distractibility among girls.

When we come to School C, however, we find different data. For one thing, the boys are very significantly less distractible than the girls, and the general trend is for more advanced students to be very significantly less distractible than the students in the earlier grades. Also, for the first time we encounter a significant interaction between the two main variables, although the level of significance is not as high as that for the two main effects. The interaction can be seen in figure 6 in the possibly out-of-line mean for tenth-grade boys and a clear crossing over of the two curves for twelfth-graders. If one looks at all the means plotted here it is clear that only four of the twelve are above 4.0, i.e., in general, social distractibility is lower in the most favored school. It will be recalled that conscientiousness was found to be greater as was denial of dislike in this same school, which reinforces the idea that lower social distractibility is a reality here. And both ideas relate to the notion of clear achievement orientation.

Figure 6
Mean Degree
of Social Distractibility

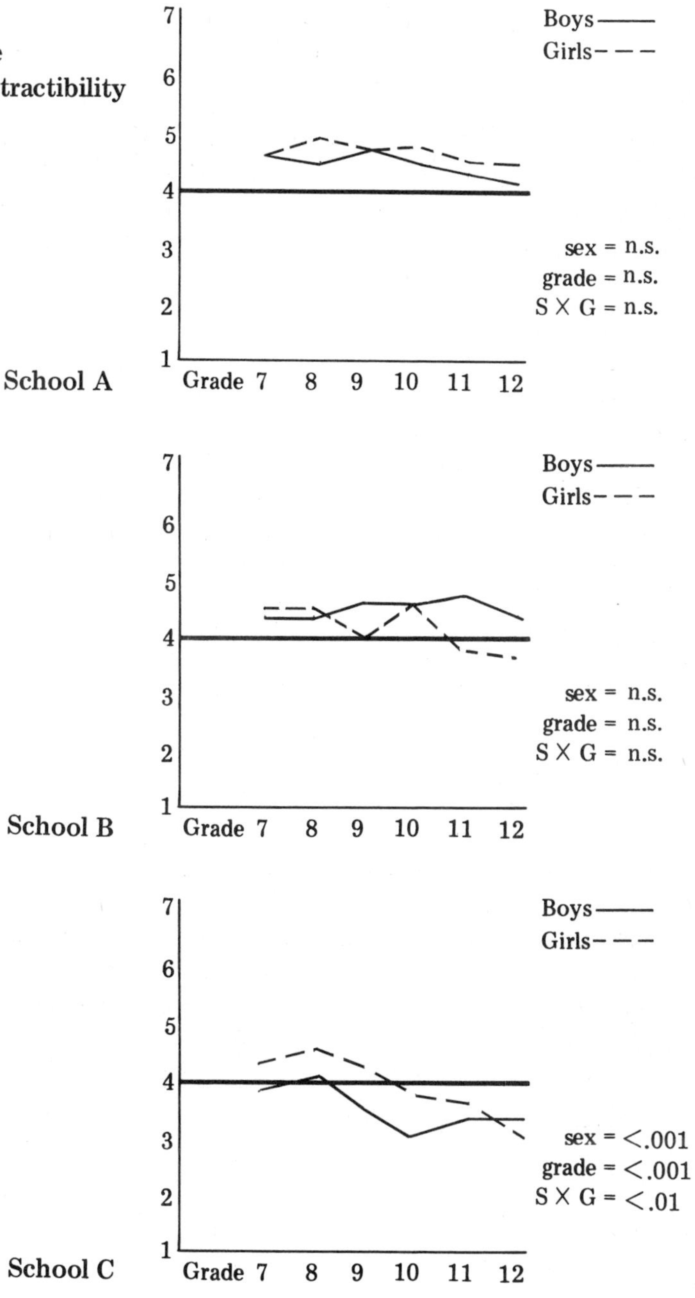
7
6
5
4
3
2
1
Boys
Girls
sex = n.s.
grade = n.s.
S X G = n.s.
School A
Grade 7 8 9 10 11 12
7
6
5
4
3
2
1
Boys
Girls
sex = n.s.
grade = n.s.
S X G = n.s.
School B
Grade 7 8 9 10 11 12
7
6
5
4
3
2
1
Boys
Girls
sex = <.001
grade = <.001
S X G = <.01
School C
Grade 7 8 9 10 11 12

When we turn to the across-schools analysis (appendix D), we see that the schools are very significantly different, and that the preceding discussion of School C is probably the explanation of the significance level. The highly significant sex difference in School C is evidently not enough to carry the day when Schools A and B are added to the analysis, for the sex variable loses all statistical significance. In contrast, the highly significant grades variation in School C evidently receives just enough support from the insignificant variations in Schools A and B that it shows up as a highly significant variation when the schools are combined; it seems difficult to me to take such a mixed finding very seriously, though this view admittedly plays down the possibility of genuine intercommunity differences.

In the across-schools analysis there are two highly significant interactions and one that does not quite reach significance. The first significant one is between schools and sex. This time, as the tabulation given below indicates, one almost has to specify a single school to learn the size and direction of a sex difference. School B shows a reversal, compared to the other schools. I cannot with confidence say what this interaction means.

	School A	*School B*	*School C*
Boys	4.5	4.4	3.7
Girls	4.6	4.2	4.0
Difference	−.1	+.2	−.3

The second significant interaction is that between schools and grades. As shown in the tabulation of weighted means below, it would appear this time that the significant effect arises primarily from the lack of systematic variation in School A, where social distractibility is almost the same in all grades, whereas in the other two schools there is decreasing social distractibility (more notably and over more grade levels in School C).

Grade	*School A*	*School B*	*School C*
7	4.6	4.4	4.1
8	4.6	4.3	4.3
9	4.7	4.2	4.1
10	4.6	4.5	3.5
11	4.5	4.2	3.6
12	4.4	4.0	3.4

Scale 7: Orientation toward the Future

This scale was constructed largely because the writings of Keniston, Erikson, and others earlier referred to agree in suggesting that an important concern of young people, particularly in later adolescence, is for what the future may bring, especially as they try to discern it in a troubled world. At the college level one of the reflections of this concern is for studies or courses which are more directly germane to the lives of the students. (This does not always symbolize a concern for the future; sometimes it represents a very different feeling—that it is simply impossible to plan for the future in such an uncertain world, so that one might as well concentrate on living here and now, and the courses demanded may be very much of that character.) At any rate, it seems of great importance that we learn how adolescents below the college level see their schooling in relation to however they view the future. With the aid of the writings of authors who have discussed this matter, it was fairly simple to invent the collection of statements (see appendix B) which make up scale 7. Some very interesting results are shown in figure 7, where we see the highest means in these studies.

In School A we find that girls are very significantly more concerned about the future than are the boys, although the boys also show strong concern on the average. The variation across grades is also significant. I suspect close study of the data will leave most people unimpressed by the significance levels. As was suggested in curves for some of the earlier scales, there is a tendency for concern to decrease during the junior high school years and then increase during senior high school. The increase in later adolescence (i.e., later grades) makes sense in this least-favored town, where one may suppose that along with all the other influences on concern for the future there is a very realistic concern among many students about "improving their lot" in the classic manner. The interaction between sex and grade is insignificant since the two sexes show about the same pattern of variation across the grades.

The difference between the sexes is highly significant in School B, but the boys, as compared to School A, have sufficiently higher means that the difference between the sexes is not very impressive

Figure 7
Mean Degree of
Orientation toward
Future

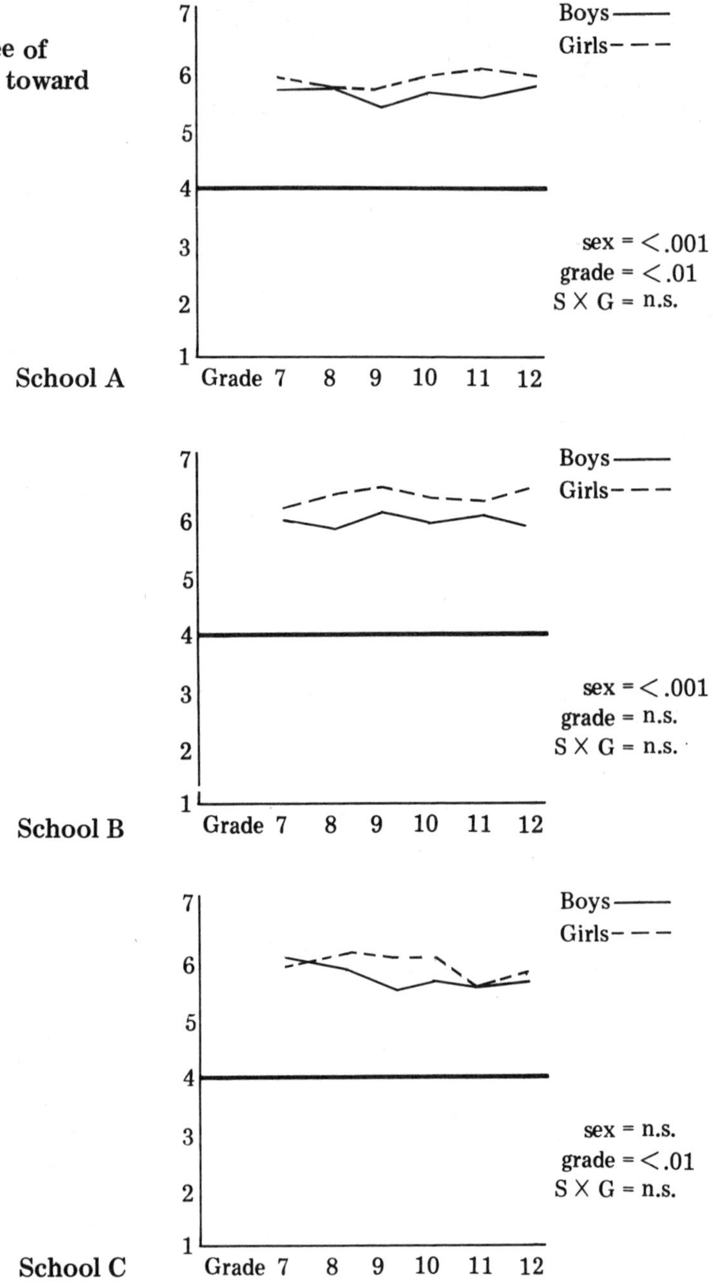

Boys———
Girls— — —

School A

sex = <.001
grade = <.01
S × G = n.s.

Boys———
Girls— — —

School B

sex = <.001
grade = n.s.
S × G = n.s.

Boys———
Girls— — —

School C

sex = n.s.
grade = <.01
S × G = n.s.

despite its statistical significance. The grade variations appear to
be random and are not significant, nor is the interaction term.
School B exhibits more of the highest means in this scale than
either of the other schools, but since all the means in each school
tend to be high, this comparison is not notably impressive.

When we turn to School C we find a somewhat different picture, as has several times been true. Here the sex difference is not
significant, and while the variation across grades does reach significance, one can find seemingly only chance variations with no
clear trend, so that this datum does not impress. There of course
is no significant interaction.

If anyone anticipated (as I did) that there would be less concern about the future in early adolescence (if only because of
heightened self-concern first being experienced), these three
graphs should serve to correct the notion. Whether one wishes
to emphasize the effects of the mass media in making people of
all ages more aware about both the present and possible future
events, or to stress the orientation of instruction and other activities in the school, or to emphasize some other factor, the data
are clear: by the time students have reached the seventh grade
they are very much concerned about the relation of their schooling to their futures.

Another intriguing point is that only in School C do the juniors
and seniors tend to decrease very notably in their concern for the
future. Why, one might ask, in a community in which it was specu-
lated that successful people would rear children who would "do as
they should," presumably including being successful in the future
as well as in school, should such a decrease in concern occur? One
can only speculate, but there is some plausibility in the idea that
the upper-grade students in such a community are, in the main,
oriented toward college or other further education, and if they
have done reasonably well in school they can feel fairly assured
that their immediate futures are secure and schooling is not cru-
cial in this sense. (These data were collected on a January 28, before seniors could have heard for sure about their acceptance into
college, so it is not possible to say that confidence about continuing education must surely have been involved.)

When we look at the across-school comparisons (appendix D)
we note that the schools differ very significantly. But since the

means for the schools are A, 5.9; B, 6.1; and C, 5.8 it seems likely that not much importance should be attached to the variations.
As has been remarked twice before, the sex difference is highly
significant except in School C, where it does not quite reach significance. I am inclined to think it probable that girls (possibly
because of greater maturity) have more concern about the future
than boys, in general. But I also feel that this statement is a very
simple introduction to what must be a very complex matter. The
only other significant variation is the interaction between schools
and grades, and although not much can be said with confidence
about this, the table of weighted means below suggests that again
School C is mainly responsible for the interaction, since it is the
only one in which the upper grades clearly tend to show less concern for the future than the lower grades included in the study.

Grade	School A	School B	School C
7	6.0	6.1	6.0
8	5.9	6.1	6.0
9	5.6	6.1	6.0
10	5.9	6.0	5.9
11	5.9	6.1	5.6
12	6.1	6.0	5.7

So many specifics have been presented in the preceding pages
that it seems desirable to review and to some extent interrelate
them. The specifics have been of three kinds. First, we have seen
the positions of many groups of students on various scales, in the
form of means purporting to show the typical strength of some
aspect of attitude toward or relevant to school. Second, we have
examined these means for (1) differences or changes in attitude
in various grade or sex groups and (2) any interaction between
sex and grade; in addition we have commented on the statistical
evaluation and in some cases the importance of differences or
variations. And third, we have when appropriate remarked on
differences among the three schools which might be related to
variations in their quality or at least to the socioeconomic and
other aspects of the communities in which they are located.

First, scale 1 (positive and active liking for school) and scale 2
(generalized dislike of school) exhibit a finding which only in
part could be anticipated on the basis of recent published commentary on schools. A dilemma exists here and requires examina-

tion. On the one hand, both sexes react the same way in rating themselves as very close to the neutral point on scale 1: they don't know whether they like school or not, which is another way of saying that most of them are apathetic or indifferent. Looking at all three schools together, one gets the impression that there may be a lessened liking as students rise above grade 7 and then a small increase, which turns out to be significant in the across-schools comparison, but this variation (in two schools of three) does not seem to be very impressive. If one looks at the results with scale 2, a curious fact is exhibited everywhere: students on the average stoutly deny that they dislike school, girls more than boys, older students somewhat more than younger ones (again, subjective judgment suggests that the latter variation is not importantly large). The possibility was suggested that the results on scale 2 are perhaps partly a function of "response set"—of not wishing to declare a number of somewhat derogatory statements to be true of one's self, even on an anonymous survey instrument. But it was also suggested that while this was possible, for the individual student it would have to govern his response to a good many statements of the scale in order to change his median position on it, so response set does not seem to be more than a partial explanation. It seems more likely that the students, with respect to school, are just there, presumably acting out what the school and their parents have taught them is expected of them. I am tempted to guess, along with some contemporary critics of schooling, that most students could not imagine life without schooling, and, even more troublesome to me, schooling of the kind they have always experienced. And for the third time it is necessary to admit that the students just may be so indifferent to school that they are being truthful when they refuse to say they dislike it.

The results with scale 3 (conscientiousness) reinforce such thinking. In all schools studied here, most subgroups are on the average conscientious, girls more so than boys and younger students more so than older ones (i.e., as maturity increases there is a lessening of the kind of conscientiousness that held students to school tasks in early adolescence). On the whole the students in the most favored school and community are more conscientious. Taken in conjunction with the results previously summarized, one gets the feeling I expressed earlier: schooling is somehow a rather joyless duty for the average student.

Scale 4 (anxiety and guilt about school) seems important to me because it has to do with the kinds of attitudes (or a species of attitude) that might work against liking school and wanting to do one's best there (that is a causal speculation). In the next chapter we shall examine a different kind of evidence to see whether it has any systematic relation to other attitudes, but in the current presentation we have only discussed its strength. As I reported earlier, the findings here confirm Sarason's finding that usually girls rate themselves higher on anxiety statements and, as one would expect, guilt statements also (Sarason's questions do not use the language of guilt, but it is implied in a good many places).

The present findings appear to extend Sarason's in two ways: first, anxiety and guilt feelings about school (which for my purposes are called attitudes) appear in both boys and girls older than those with whom Sarason worked, suggesting that the possible suppression of anxiety which he thought was causing sex differences especially in the older children he worked with is here "released" to some degree by the method of anonymous self-rating. Second, in girls as well as boys, there is a gradual trend toward *not* rating one's self as anxious or guilty the further through school (adolescence) the average student goes. A final point about the anxiety and guilt findings here is that they do not conform to my expectation that in an affluent and successful community there would be extra pressures on children to succeed, with accompanying fear of failure on their part; instead, on the average, students in the affluent community show lower scores on scale 4 than do students in the other two school systems. To turn the statement around, they appear to be more secure and less concerned. I cannot objectively evaluate this further, as indicated earlier, because my expectation was formed at a time when I was using only single statements, not scales, and because I did not gather preliminary information in schools similar to A and B. But I could not avoid the possibly extreme speculation that if community C is an achievement-oriented community, as there are signs it is, admissions of anxiety or guilt about school are more completely suppressed here than even in the communities in which I gathered preliminary data.

I suspect there is some comfort to be taken from the results from scale 5 (favorable attitude toward teachers), at least by teachers. The rather widely held belief that adolescents can say little good about teachers (which is interpreted by some as meaning that teachers are authoritarian, parentlike figures) is contradicted by the results in all three school systems studied here: students on the average like teachers, girls somewhat more than boys, and older students seemingly more than younger ones, although the latter finding is not impressively clear. Some interesting possibilities of interpretation reside in these results. One is that the presumed dislike of teachers is "public talk" intended for other adults or other adolescents. If it is simply the thing to say, in the security of anonymity students don't rate themselves this way. Another speculation is that the increase in liking for teachers among older students that is significant in the across-schools analysis could be related to the relatively more common existence of male teachers in the high school and perhaps in the junior high. (Variations across the grades were unimpressive in size, it is necessary to remember.) And finally, for those who have believed adolescents do not like teachers, there is the possibility (resembling what I have said previously in other connections) that teachers do as they are expected. This is the only context in which the students know them, and teachers are liked for the way they are doing what is expected of them. Indeed, the students would be dismayed if they behaved in any other way.

Scale 6 (social distractibility) shows that in schools A and B the typical student (except for girls in grades 9, 11, and 12, School B) is somewhat distractible by his peers or friends. But the students in School C are clearly different—they are in general less distractible, just as they more strongly denied disliking school and rated themselves as more conscientious. Girls are more distractible than boys on the average (until grade 12), and distractibility decreases as each sex passes further through adolescence. The latter finding at first glance seems somewhat contrary to the finding that conscientiousness gradually decreases during the same period. Study of the content of the scales (appendix B), however, reveals that the measure of conscientiousness is almost entirely oriented toward this trait defined as personal or individual behavior, whereas the social distractibility statements almost of necessity have to do with the student's relations with other students. In the next chapter we shall examine data bearing on the question of whether the two attitudes are in fact different or are merely the same thing measured in two different ways.

One more remark seems pertinent about School C and the ways it has thus far differed from the other two schools. The attitudinal differences suggest that the students of School C are perhaps more strongly achievement-oriented, a general label for the greater denial of dislike for school, the higher level of conscientiousness, and now the lower degree of social distractibility. Being achievement-oriented does not necessarily mean that one likes the task in which one is set to achieve; in fact, achievement-orientation often carries a person through a task which is not pleasing but which is necessary on the way to some further goal.

The last of our scales is number 7 (orientation toward the future): It shows to an impressive degree that in the seventh grade and thereafter the students are much concerned about the pertinence of schooling to their futures. As a matter of statistical reality, the means are so close to the upper end of the scale that it is a little surprising to find there are variations between the sexes (highly significant in Schools A and B, not in School C) and across the grades (except in School B). While it is interesting to speculate about what appears to be a slight decrease in concern for the future in the junior high and a slight increase in senior high in School A, in relation to the theme of "improving one's lot in the world," the surest point is that through some of many influences—mass media, the orientation of the schools, the home—by the time they reach seventh grade students have become much concerned about the relation of their schooling to the future. Perhaps this is another factor holding them in school even when they are not willing to say they like it.

Finally, it seems realistic to say that although there were significant variations among the three school systems selected because they were deemed to vary widely in quality or in the socioeconomic status of the community and therefore in the kinds of peers the students probably had, the overall impression one gets repeatedly is one of similarity among strengths and changes in student attitudes. It is true that School C was most often deviant from the others, but not in any consistent pattern. One can only guess that the conceptions of school held by students are homogeneous to an unexpected degree.

8. PATTERNS OF ADOLESCENT ATTITUDES
TOWARD SCHOOL

The preceding discussion has emphasized the strength of any given attitude among different grade-level groups and the two sexes separately, with a view to finding out not only how strong the attitudes are but whether they are predominantly antischool or proschool and whether they change as students of differing grade-level are asked for their self-ratings. As an added fillip the question was raised whether the quality of the school, or the kind of community it exists in, is related to the kinds of attitudes students have. Now we turn to a quite different emphasis: the ways in which attitudes toward school (or related to school) are patterned.

We can talk about patterning in two ways: (1) How do attitudes correlate with one another (for correlation coefficients will be our primary source of information)? and (2) What is the structure of attitudes toward school? The expression "personality structure" is very often used, but to me it implies a broader picture of the make-up of a person or persons than can be formulated in the rather limited area of this study, and so I shall refer usually to the patterning of the attitudes measured here. The term "pattern" will be rather arbitrarily defined to mean any set of attitudes that correlate positively with each other and simultaneously correlate negatively or at a low level with other sets of attitudes. (It could be argued with some force that sets of attitudes correlating positively with each other and equally negatively with attitudes in another set are in fact members of a more inclusive bipolar pattern, from a statistical point of view. Here, however, it seems simpler to use the formulation given previously.)

We should not underestimate the importance of knowing about the patterning of attitudes related to school. School occupies much of the adolescent's time and energy, and society has assigned a good many responsibilities to the school for the development of the adolescent (whether it is competent to bear all these responsibilities or not). Furthermore, student reactions to school, as we have already seen, are by no means uniform and may indeed reflect considerable conflict within individuals or between students and the schools they are in. It must be added, however, that several of the attitudes measured here (e.g., anxiety or conscientiousness) may readily be conceived of as very general in the lives of individuals, so that their reactions to school are but reflections of behavior patterning that pervades much or most of their daily lives.

The data forming the basis of this discussion are primarily the intercorrelations (*r*s) of the scales, i.e., within any one of the 12 subgroups of a school system the individual supplies us with his scores on each of two scales, and all such pairs of scores within the subgroup are used in computing the correlation between the scales. The 126 *r*s for each sex in each school system are recorded in appendix E for specific reference. For only one purpose shall I refer directly to the data in that appendix; for all other purposes I shall average the *r*s across grade levels within a sex within a school system, to produce tables which are more readable and which allow easier comparison of schools.

Three general statements of caution concerning the study of these *r*s seem necessary. The first is that, as was said in relation to the earlier analysis of variance, the numbers of students within most of the subgroups are large enough so that an *r* may appear very significant statistically, even though for either practical or theoretical purposes it may not be important. A second caution is that one must always remember that *r*s merely tell us the degree to which scores on two scales vary together: does a high score on one scale tend to be paired with a high one, a low one, or a randomly located one along the other scale? An *r* may lead us to speculate about causal relations among attitudes or traits, but it does not permit us to draw any conclusions whatever about causality. (The causality statement comes most directly from experiments in which independent variables are deliberately manipulated to determine whether they are systematically related to changes in supposed dependent variables.) The third thing to remember is that *r*s only tell us about degree of relationship; they say nothing about means (which were the object of the analyses of variance reported earlier). Thus, a group may have a high mean score on one attitude and a low mean score on another (as extremes, take any group in any school and look back to its mean on the scale measuring attitude toward the future and its mean on the dislike scale). Such a difference in means does not tell us, as *r*s are intended to, whether the students rating themselves high on one of those scales tend to be the ones rating themselves high on the other, or whether some other pattern is found when the actual *r* is computed.

Shown in table 2 are the *r*s averaged across grades within each school, for each scale paired with every other scale, within each school, for boys only. We shall look with care at these *r*s, for as the footnote to table 2 shows, only four fail to be significant at the *p*<.01 level of significance. We shall begin the study of this table by systematically examining the relationships of each scale with each of the others in turn. Then we can begin the search for patterns of relationships, which will help to organize and simplify our understanding.

I earlier pointed out that the scales measuring positive and active liking for school and generalized dislike for school contained different kinds of statements and thus seemed to be tapping different aspects of attitude toward school. Nevertheless, it appears from the first three entries in table 2 that there is a clear tendency for students rating themselves high on one scale to rate themselves low on the other and vice versa. The highest *r*s in the entire table are found between liking for school and conscientiousness about schoolwork. It is an interesting (but causal) speculation that such *r*s occur because child-rearing practices or school experiences that produce liking for school simultaneously produce conscientiousness toward it. (The reverse statement of course must be made about students at the other end of each distribution.) Another interesting fact is that liking for school is positively correlated, at a rather low level to be sure, with anxiety and guilt feelings about school. More about this later. It is not surprising to observe next that there is a clear tendency for those who like school better to like teachers better, nor is it surprising that they are less readily distracted from their schoolwork. Finally, the students who like school better tend to be more concerned about their futures.

If we now move down in table 2 to the *r*s with generalized dis-

Table 2. Intercorrelations of the Seven Scales Based on Averages
across Grade Levels in Schools A, B, and C, Boys Only

	Schools	Generalized dislike	Conscientiousness	Anxiety-guilt	Liking for teachers	Social distractibility	Orientation toward future
Positive and active liking	A	−.38	+.63	+.22	+.45	−.28	+.40
	B	−.36	+.52	+.17	+.37	−.24	+.33
	C	−.39	+.52	+.07	+.44	−.20	+.41
Generalized dislike	A		−.45	.00	−.44	+.49	−.45
	B		−.42	+.02	−.41	+.51	−.45
	C		−.44	+.14	−.50	+.45	−.52
Conscientiousness	A			+.21	+.50	−.34	+.45
	B			+.21	+.50	−.34	+.45
	C			+.15	+.40	−.30	+.53
Anxiety-guilt	A				+.16	+.10	+.15
	B				+.16	+.14	+.19
	C				−.04	+.23	+.11
Liking for teachers	A					−.27	+.43
	B					−.27	+.43
	C					−.29	+.46
Social distractibility	A						−.27
	B						−.25
	C						−.27

School	n	$p < .01$
A	843	.09
B	477	.12
C	826	.09

like for school, we find first an expected set of *r*s, negative in sign and fairly sizable, with conscientiousness about schoolwork. But then we find that dislike for school is not clearly related to anxiety and guilt feelings about it. At the intuitive level this is somewhat surprising, to me at least, for I expected the two scales to show definite positive *r*s. (This does not imply that anxiety and guilt *cause* dislike of school, or vice versa; the statement leaves open and unsettled many possible explanations of relationship, such as a student's feeling anxious *and* disliking school because he knows his talents for schoolwork are not great.) It is not surprising that students who tend to dislike school tend not to like teachers, nor is it remarkable that they have a clear tendency to be socially distractible, i.e., escape from their schoolwork. Finally, there appears to be an unhappy and clear tendency for those who dislike school more to be less concerned about the relation of schooling to their future.

Going now to the rows labeled conscientiousness, we discover first nearly zero positive *r*s with anxiety and guilt feelings. It has long been assumed by many personality theorists that conscientiousness has much of its basis in early punishment, anxiety, and guilt, so it might well be expected that a positive relationship would turn up here. Conscientiousness is also positively related to liking for teachers and, as one would predict, negatively related to social distractibility. It clearly correlates positively with orientation toward the future, suggesting that the two may have some common roots.

As seen in the next rows in table 2 and in the relevant column, the scale measuring anxiety and guilt correlates less closely with other scales on the average than does any other scale used here. Except for the possible relationship with conscientiousness there is no consistent group of very close *r*s with any other variable. Furthermore, the tendency toward positive *r*s with liking for teachers and orientation toward the future seem rather more like coincidence than anything of theoretical significance. It is as though degree of anxiety or guilt is a factor pervading many of an individual's activities to some degree, and only some of the attitudes toward school measured here relate to sources of anxiety, or reflect them.

As to the last three sets of *r*s in table 2, we need only note that
from what we have said above it is not surprising that liking for
teachers correlates negatively with social distractibility and positively with concern for the relation of schooling to the future.
And social distractibility correlates negatively with each attitude
that correlates positively with concern for the future, so logically it should be negatively related to concern for the future as it
indeed is.

Now can we discern any organizing and simplifying ideas or
patterns among the 21 sets of *r*s which we have examined in some
detail? There do indeed seem to be two sets of attitude measures
which correlate positively with each other within groups and
negatively or at a low level with every measure in the other
group. That is, liking for school, conscientiousness, liking for
teachers, and orientation toward the future correlate positively
in every possible pair. Another positive correlation is found between dislike for school and social distractibility. These latter
two attitudes relate either negatively with each attitude in the
first group or, with two exceptions on different traits in different schools, at a low level.

The one attitude not fitting clearly or neatly into either of the
two major patterns is anxiety-guilt. I have said it would be psychologically meaningful to take seriously the *r*s with conscientiousness, for many personality theorists have considered conscientiousness to have some of its roots in, or take some of its motive
power from, feelings of anxiety and guilt. If we did take this
possible relationship seriously in these data, and the pattern of
attitudes including conscience is thought to be real, we should
expect to find anxiety-guilt correlated with liking for school,
liking for teachers, and orientation toward the future. In every
instance there are positive correlations but mostly small ones.
For now it seems desirable not to make claims about anxiety
and guilt feelings as belonging to the attitude pattern named.
The same must be said for the relation of such feelings to the
dislike-social distractibility pattern. We shall see in a moment
whether this is different when we discuss the data for girls.

Finally we might raise a question which table 2 cannot answer
and for which we must refer to appendix E. The question is
whether the size of *r*s between scales (i.e., nature of attitude

patterning) changes as grade-level (stage of adolescence) changes. The simplest way of answering this question is to tabulate, in appendix E, the differences between the grades in such a way as to show how frequently (in how many of the 21 sets of comparisons per school) the twelfth grade r is larger or smaller than that for the seventh grade. This is suggested because, in appendix E, one can readily see that for a good many of the comparisons, the correlations seem to be lessening in size with increased grade level. The suggested test, while simple, has the shortcoming that it utilizes only part of the available data and thus may be erratic.

In School A the tabulation just proposed leads to a count of 16 instances in which the twelfth grade r is smaller and 5 in which it is not or the results are ambiguous. By a simple chi-square test this difference is significant at less than the .01 level. The scale on which the decrease is most often ambiguous or reversed is that for anxiety-guilt. When we turn to School B, the number of times the twelfth grade correlation is unambiguously smaller than the seventh is but 9 out of 21. Anxiety again intercorrelates in seemingly random variations with other scales as grade level changes. All in all, this school does not show the same results as School A. When we turn to School C, however, we find a slightly more extreme form of the tendency for rs to decrease as grade level rises. In 17 of the 21 possible comparisons, the twelfth grade r is smaller than the seventh, a result significant at less than the .001 level. In School C the anxiety scale is again the "different" one with respect to changes across grade level.

What are we to make of all this? School B clearly is in a class by itself, in that the simple but rather insensitive tabulation I used shows no systematic change across grade levels. Schools A and C, however, show such a change at a respectable level of significance, even with an insensitive test. I suspect that the latter two schools are showing us what we ought to see, in the sense that the trends they show in the relationships among scales as students become more mature on the average have been found in a good many realms of personality and ability research: as a person develops, some of his various traits and talents reach different stable levels, but he continues to develop in other ways, and the result is in general a decrease in rs among many of his talents and traits. This effect has been termed individuation—

the person is becoming more individualized as he develops (see Allport 1967, p. 108 and elsewhere). I have no idea why the data from School B do not support such an interpretation. The number of ambiguities and reversals involving anxiety-guilt again suggests that this variable should be considered apart from the others.

Now let us turn to table 3, another condensation of data from appendix E obtained by averaging *r*s between attitudes for grades 7-12 inclusive, but this time for the girls only. We shall follow the same discussion sequence as for the boys' data, but the results are so impressively similar for the two sexes that the girls' data will receive less attention.

Among the girls, liking for school correlates negatively with dislike, positively with conscientiousness, positively with feelings of anxiety and guilt about school, positively with liking for teachers, negatively with social distractibility and positively with liking for teachers, and negatively with social distractibility and positively with orientation toward the future. With such large samples of students being involved, if these were correlations computed on each whole sample, the resultant coefficients would almost all be highly significant statistically (see footnote to table 3). Dislike for school again correlates negatively with conscientiousness, possibly positively with anxiety-guilt, negatively with liking for teachers, positively with social distractibility, and negatively with concern for the future, which seems as regrettable here as it did for the boys.

Conscientiousness also produces results consistent with those among boys. It correlates positively but not closely with anxiety-guilt, quite positively with liking for teachers, rather negatively with social distractibility, and quite positively with concern for the future. Anxiety and guilt feelings show a low and somewhat mixed relationship to liking for teachers. Anxiety and guilt feelings correlate positively but at a low level with social distractibility. They correlate at a low level and with varying algebraic signs with concern for the future. Liking for teachers correlates only modestly and negatively with social distractibility, and fairly clearly and positively with concern for the future. Finally, social distractibility correlates negatively and at a modest level with concern for the future.

In our efforts to simplify this information, we see that the girls'

Table 3. Intercorrelations of the Seven Scales Based on Averages
across Grade Levels in Schools A, B, and C, Girls Only

	Schools	Generalized dislike	Conscientiousness	Anxiety-guilt	Liking for teachers	Social distractibility	Orientation toward future
Positive and active liking	A	-.40	+.62	+.16	+.48	-.35	+.38
	B	-.41	+.55	+.09	+.44	-.28	+.43
	C	-.30	+.50	+.02	+.40	-.20	+.33
Generalized dislike	A		-.53	-.03	-.49	+.42	-.53
	B		-.43	+.08	-.48	+.43	-.52
	C		-.45	+.09	-.41	+.39	-.46
Conscientiousness	A			+.20	+.47	-.39	+.48
	B			+.11	+.43	-.34	+.44
	C			+.15	+.36	-.27	+.45
Anxiety-guilt	A				+.17	+.08	+.09
	B				+.07	+.08	+.07
	C				+.02	+.21	+.05
Liking for teachers	A					-.28	+.43
	B					-.27	+.41
	C					-.22	+.41
Social distractibility	A						-.28
	B						-.20
	C						-.21

School	n	p=<.01
A	976	.08
B	491	.12
C	820	.09

data, as already mentioned, yield almost the same patterns of attitudes as did those of the boys. First, as for the boys, there appears to be a pattern of attitudes which correlates positively with each other and negatively with the others. This pattern again includes liking for school, conscientiousness, liking for teachers, and concern for the future, but the rs are inconsistent and low with feelings of anxiety and guilt. The inclusion of the latter attitude in this factor does not seem very reasonable. The second grouping consists, again, of the two other scales: dislike for school and social distractibility correlate quite definitely and positively with each other and negatively, usually to a fair degree, with the other variables except anxiety-guilt. We see also among the girls an inconsistent relationship of anxiety-guilt with other variables. We therefore cannot escape the idea that dividing our two tables of intercorrelations into two groups may be a bit simplistic or at least incomplete: feelings of anxiety and guilt may both draw the student to his schoolwork and repel him from it, or, to avoid this language of causality, the anxiety-guilt attitude is possibly part of both clusters we find. It may even be a factor standing by itself.

When we again refer to appendix E and use the tallying procedure of testing to see whether changes in size of r occur across grade levels, we find about the same results as with boys. In School A, the tallies are identical with those for boys; in B there is no discernible pattern; and in School C the variation is again significant at less than the .01 level. For the girls as well as for the boys, therefore, it seems that we might well disregard School B and interpret the decreasing rs of attitudes as a sign of individuation during adolescence.

In summary, I will remark on what appear to be the four generalized ideas we may draw from the combined tables, i.e., taking the two sexes together.

The first idea is that several of the attitudes measured here seem to group themselves together, as shown by rs in the three schools. It seems very probable that liking for school, conscientiousness, liking for teachers, and concern for the future relate positively to each other in all three schools. It also seems probable that dislike for school and social distractibility form a smaller cluster which correlates negatively or at a low level with the first-named group. Anxiety and guilt feelings are a debatable case in this analysis, for there is some evidence that not only are they related to the pattern of "positive" attitudes, but also to the "negative" attitudes. In each case, inclusion of the variable is, at least in a tentative way, psychologically sensible for somewhat different reasons. And it could be argued that anxiety-guilt should stand by itself. Only when knowledge about attitudes toward school becomes more complete and detailed can this statement be adequately tested.

The second general idea arising in the examination of these data is that the attitudes measured here intercorrelate more closely in the early years of adolescence (lower grades) than they do later. This is said in deliberate disregard of the data from School B, in which this pattern is not really discernible for unknown reasons. Perhaps the main reason I wish to make this generalization is that the process of individuation is widely considered to be part of the process of development, and I see no convincing reason why it should not, by a ratio of two schools to one, be regarded as exhibited here.

The third generalization can be stated briefly: the quality of school, or of the community in which it exists, bears no clear relationship to the detailed interrelationships of attitudes measured here, or to the tentative clustering of attitudes which was discussed above.

And fourth, with the exception of the reservations expressed above concerning how to fit anxiety and guilt into the patterns of attitudes, for which the evidence was slightly different for each sex, all other aspects of attitude patterning were the same for the sexes. It was only in the earlier analyses of intensity of attitudes that the sexes differed rather consistently.

9. ANOTHER COMPONENT OF ATTITUDE
AND A REPLICATION

We have seen, as we have been led to expect by almost every historical comment on school we have read, that there are many students who do not like school. It is reasonable to say that we do not know very well why this is so: are the students led to expect to feel this way by their parents (who may have felt the same way) or by their friends, or is it that what happens to them in school leaves them cool toward the whole idea of schooling? In the results reported here thus far we have seen that the only mean responses of mainly favorable reaction to any aspect of school are those toward teachers, the relation of schooling to the future, and conscientiousness about schoolwork. It is true that in general, social distractibility and anxiety were above the neutral point as measured by the scales used here, but mainly I regard these as undesirable aspects of attitude toward school itself. The odd thing is that the students quite uniformly (on the average) rated themselves as indifferent on the scale measuring liking for school, then firmly denied that they dislike school, and then said they are conscientious. In each of the scales used, there were significant across-school variations reflecting differences in sex, grade, socioeconomic status or quality, or, in a few cases, interactions of two of these variables. I have reviewed these specific details and shall not repeat them here. In any case, I find the similarities among schools more impressive than the differences. It is the overall view of student attitude thus far described which is puzzling; it is not only that the attitudes of many students in certain respects are probably not conducive to good motivation toward learning, but that within themselves they seem in certain ways inconsistent. It is not sufficient to dismiss this by saying, "What else do you expect of adolescents?" because it is precisely this mix of attitudes that needs to be better understood by those who deal with adolescents in school, or by adolescents themselves.

In my earlier discussions it was implicit that students will learn when they are interested and nothing interferes. John Dewey did

not invent that idea but he did much to explicate it before others
began to distort and overextend it. I should like to make clear my
own feeling that the current formal analyses of the learning process by psychologists do not help much in understanding learning
in school. We can, of course, learn something from certain aspects
of formal learning theories, such as intrinsic and extrinsic motives
(originating within the learner or outside) and intrinsic and extrinsic rewards. But learning in school may be influenced in
what for now must be mainly unexplicated ways, unless we
learn more about attitudes (which I place in the general category
of motives), conflicts among attitudes toward school, conflicts
of school-related attitudes with non-school-related attitudes, and
attitudes about other everyday aspects of living and schooling.
In this study the complex of attitudes which seems to me of particular importance to understand is that consisting of liking for
school, dislike of school, and conscientiousness, as mentioned
above. For reasons not readily apparent to me, the fact that so
many students rate themselves low on liking for school that the
mean is near the indifference point is perhaps the "fact" most
urgently in need of understanding, especially when it is accompanied
by a denial of dislike for school and, thus far, self-ratings of definite
conscientiousness.

Purpose of a second study

As I discussed the findings reported thus far with my colleagues
and students and extended the range of my readings I became
convinced that at least one essential attitude scale had been
omitted. This one should attempt to measure attitude toward
the way the school operates or is organized, or the way it influences the lives of adults and students who are there. This has nothing to do with physical plant (which was good or very good in
Schools A, B, and C), but with what *happens* in that place, other
than academic or skills learning, that involves any combination of
administration, teachers, or students. I might put it this way: how
does the school as a social system function with regard to all the
different personalities in it, the assigned or assumed roles they
play, and the interrelationships among all these as social beings
or involvements? Anyone who has spent very much time in a
school knows that, whether or not it is made explicit (it usually

is), certain norms are set for the conduct of students and faculty
alike, certain social relationships are known or taught, and certain
tasks are to be accomplished—typically by a set time in a set way.
The school is full of "do's" and "don'ts."
Since this general study deals with pre-adolescents and adolescents, people who, as was said at greater length in Part 1 of this
book, are seeking autonomy, self-determination, individuality, and
so on, it seems desirable to find out whether they accept the school
as it is, or whether as a social system the school is, or becomes,
contrary to the personal aspirations and the behavioral tenden-
cies of those who are simultaneously passing through adolescence
and through school.

A new attitude scale

It will be remembered that approximately 100 statements seemed
to be the maximum that I could expect the younger students and
the school itself to permit me to use in the amount of time that
could reasonably be given to a single piece of research. To add a
new scale it was therefore necessary to shorten each of the seven
scales enough to permit the addition of a whole new set of statements. This dictated that eight 12-item scales be used. Of the original seven scales, five in their final form contained 13 or 14 items,
and it was a simple task to search out the earlier item analyses
and discard either one or two of the less closely correlated statements to make each of these five scales into a 12-item scale. The
scales measuring liking for teachers and social distractibility in
their final form had contained only 11 items and in addition were
the least reliable of the seven scales. It was therefore decided to
do a trial run with a set of statements including possible improve-
ments on or additions to these two original scales and a fairly
generous number of statements from among which to select by
item analysis the 12 to make up the new scale.

The trial-run questionnaire then consisted of the standard cover
page of instructions and in addition 15 statements retained or added
as possibly measuring attitude toward teachers, 15 concerning social distractibility, and 18 statements supposedly measuring attitude toward the school as a social system, assembled in random
order. It was administered to a sample of 120 students spread
over grades 7 through 12 in School D, and the item analyses were

performed on the entire sample. The two original scales were, on
this basis, not only extended to 12 items, but revised in a few
cases to replace earlier statements with seemingly more appropriate ones. The wholly new scale, of course, consisted of those
12 statements among the 18 which exhibited closest correlations
of individual statements with all remaining items in the group.
(None of the exact statements or data involved in this preliminary
run is recorded here, since they merely led to the final form of
measuring instrument concerning which all data are recorded.
See appendix F for the revised set of seven scales plus the new
one, and appendix G for the questionnaire into which they were
formed by the random-number-table procedure described previously.)

The "new" questionnaire and the situation

There are five aspects of what will be reported in the following
sections that deserve prior attention. First, although I will compare results in School D with those in systems discussed earlier,
these comparisons cannot be taken as exact, for not only were
all the scales slightly modified or new for school D, but they were
assembled by the random-number system and most statements
therefore appeared in a different order from the scales used in
the earlier schools. That is, the context, or surround, of each
statement was, in unspecifiable ways, different in the "new"
questionnaire. The second (and apparently trivial) point is that
I had found that even slow seventh-grade readers seemingly had
no trouble with the questionnaire in previous schools when the
numbers they circled ranged from +3 through 0 to - 3, which required my adding +4 to each answer to give every response a positive algebraic sign for computer purposes. This time, therefore,
I switched to a line of numbers ranging from 7 (defined as "very
true of me") through 4 ("don't know," "in between") to 1
("very untrue of me"). The students gave no indication that this
was troublesome, and, of course, the saving in coding time was
tremendous. Administration of the questionnaires was handled
as before.

The third point to be mentioned concerns the reliabilities of
the scales in their final form. These were computed by the method
described earlier and the reliability of the full length of scale again

estimated by the Spearman-Brown Prophecy Formula. In appendix
H the reliability of each scale as it functioned in each of the 12 subgroups (6 grades, 2 sexes) is shown. The average across grades
may suffice for report here: positive and active liking for school,
.74; generalized dislike for school, .71; conscientiousness, .78;
anxiety and guilt about school, .70; favorable attitude toward
teachers, .59; social distractibility, .61; orientation toward the
future, .50; favorable attitude toward the school as a social system, .62. Only the scale concerned with attitude toward the future gives cause for concern; that it should be so low is unexpected and unexplained, for in Schools A, B, and C the average
reliability of this scale was .67. Inspection of the entire table of
96 coefficients in appendix H shows only one serious problem:
the reliability of the scale just mentioned was uniquely low (.13)
among eleventh-grade boys. One can place little confidence in any
data from that particular scale in that particular group.

Fourth, the nature of the school and community should be
known, at least in the general way the earlier research sites were
described. School D, according to the fact sheet prepared by the
guidance department of the high school, is described as being in
a middle-income suburb near the medium-sized city mentioned in
relation to Schools A and B. (I learned from census data published
in the newspapers that all four communities have an almost minis-
cule proportion of nonwhite residents.) The residents, as they
are known to the school, are mainly business, professional, and
skilled laboring people. It is perhaps an unmeasured bit higher in
socioeconomic class on the average than community B, but it
very definitely is not up to community C in this regard. The high
school is comprehensive, with a considerable proportion of students electing vocational or general curricula. Modular scheduling
is employed in the high school. (Module length is 20 minutes,
and a wide variety of combinations of these units may be used
in arranging the work of a particular student for greatest effec-
tiveness.) Unscheduled time may be spent in resource centers, the
library, or independent study, and in areas of the curriculum students might not otherwise experience. There are several electives
in English during senior year, and these change from year to year.
Similarly there are several senior-year electives in social studies,
and a variety of levels of work in foreign languages, beginning in

junior high school. Advanced mathematics courses are available, as are such subjects as economics or pre-engineering graphics. From the point of view of curriculum, then, School D bears more resemblance to School C than to any other, but it is not so advanced or so complex in the resources it makes available. About half the 1971 graduating class took the Scholastic Aptitude Tests in 1970, and the mean results were: boys verbal, 473; boys mathematical, 494; girls verbal, 479; girls mathematical, 462. In this comparison, School D falls somewhat below School B. A list of colleges attended by the class of 1970, together with numbers of students at each institution, shows a rather wide range, including several of the most or next-most prestigious undergraduate institutions in the country. A conspicuous number of the graduates attended in-state institutions, particularly the state colleges. An unclear impression can be formed that School B is somewhat exceeded in its college attendance record by School D but that the latter is definitely not up to School C.

An official of the School D, not the principal, was of the impression that the teachers were trained in a wide variety of institutions and that many held masters degrees because of the close proximity of a state college which makes part-time study feasible; this same official indicated that the rate of pupil turnover was less than 1 percent per year and that the rate of teacher turnover was quite small. I thus form the impression that of the school systems previously studied, School D is most like School B. This close a replication of schools, granting that exact replication is impossible, is in this case fortunate, for if you will recall earlier discussions, it was School B that occasionally yielded results somewhat at variance with one or both of the other schools. Thus, we may perhaps clarify our opinions about students' attitudes in a system which is at neither extreme on the socioeconomic scale or, if you will, the quality-of-school scale.

Finally, a word should be said about problems confronted in collecting data in School D. As was indicated in the general discussion of such problems, they occurred in all schools reported on. But one problem seemed, subjectively and objectively, to be exacerbated in School D. This was the higher frequency of unusable papers from boys in grades 8, 11, and 12, because of failure to complete the questionnaire. That there sometimes was

outright anger, either at the statements the students were asked
to rate themselves on (rarely expressed in the other schools) or
at the idea of being asked to take "another test," was made abun-
dantly clear by the remarks, often of a contemporary obscene
sort, written on the papers by those who refused to complete
them. (Once in a while a girl also showed hostility—but *very*
rarely.) Some students wrote critical remarks and went ahead to
complete the paper satisfactorily, but as far as I could tell, in
these three grades I "lost" more papers because of negative reactions than ever before, perhaps a maximum of 10 percent
more. Unfortunately, since the likelihood is that these students
were among those who would have rated themselves low on such
scales as liking for school or conscientiousness, or high on the dislike scale, there is a definite possibility that the computed means
in these three groups are in error in the direction that would
make them appear more favorable toward school. One could at
least make a subjective allowance for this (and I have tried to
do so) in the results for certain scales, but on others (e.g., anxiety-
guilt feelings) it is difficult to guess whether those who exploded
in anger were extremely anxious people in school, or could so ex-
plode because they were not anxious about school or the consequences of any expression of opinion or feeling. I perhaps should
include the subjective impression, which has to remain that way
because it did not develop until after a number of the discarded
papers had been lost (to a Volunteer Fireman's paper-drive), that
a high proportion of those whose papers were incomplete or otherwise unusable "broke down" when they encountered one too many
statements concerning anxiety. However, this would require special
investigation because it is also true that School D has a considerable amount of interaction with Yale, and its students may have
acquired both the attitude toward tests and the language they
used from university-level friends and acquaintances. At any
rate, a total of 2067 papers were fully usable. (After this was
written, the junior- and senior-high principals sensibly pointed
out that there might be a special effect of having two grades per
building: in grade 8, the boys are said to tend toward "saltiness";
in grades 9 and 10 nothing special happens; in grades 11 and 12
more boys may feel the need to prove their independence.)

The First Seven Scales

Before we analyze the results of the new scale (number 8), it will be of general interest to determine whether School D replicates the results obtained in the first three schools for the seven scales the separate studies have approximately in common. If indeed the results seem similar we may take the results of measurement with the new scale somewhat more seriously than otherwise. (It of course would be desirable to replicate the use of the new scale, or the whole new questionnaire, but exploratory studies have to stop somewhere, some time, and at some financial limit.) The discussions of the first seven scales will be relatively brief, so that our judgments of the comparability of School D to the others, or the new questionnaire to the earlier one, will be based on highlights rather than exhaustive comparison. Exact data are recorded in appendix I.

Positive and active liking for school

As is shown in figure 8, in only one comparison of the sexes is there more than .1 of a scale step between the means, and the statistical evaluation says just that: the sex difference is insignificant, as in the other three schools. On the other hand, the

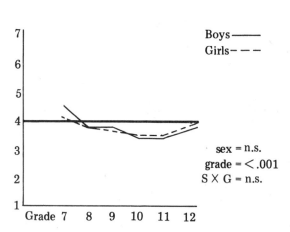

Figure 8
Mean Degree of Positive
and Active Liking

Boys ———
Girls – – –

sex = n.s.
grade = <.001
S X G = n.s.

School D   Grade 7   8   9   10   11   12

variation across grades is highly significant, and since this is the third school of four (School B is the exception) in which this has appeared, I am about ready to believe in it, small though the actual effect is. It appears that, with some variation from school to school, there is a slight decrease in liking for school beginning after grade seven, and then, at some later grade level a reversal, most clearly in senior year. Since both sexes show approximately the same thing, the S x G interaction is insignificant.

What makes School D seem similar to the first three most clearly, however, is that the means for liking of school hover around 4.0, even though the trend mentioned above may be present, i.e., in School D as elsewhere the students are unwilling to rate themselves, on the average, as liking school. It should be remarked, although not with technical certainty, that the scores on liking for school are very slightly lower, on the whole, than in any of the other schools.

Generalized dislike of school

To my surprise, when an item analysis was again done on the 12 supposedly "good" statements of this scale (they had survived three previous analyses), two statements had to be discarded, so this became a 10-statement scale. The findings (see figure 9) are about as they were in the previous schools: the girls deny disliking school significantly more than do the boys; there is a significant variation across grades, consisting of an early decrease in strength of denial and in later grades a stronger denial again; and both sexes show this so the S x G interaction is insignificant.

As before, we have the paradox that although on the average the students are rather close to the indifference point on the liking scale, they are well below it on the dislike scale. Although the means for boys in grades 8, 11, and 12 may be in error by some unknown amount, it would appear here, as in figure 8, that the curves do not show strange fluctuations for these groups, nor does the difference between curves for boys and girls show any conspicuous variation at these points. All in all, then, it would appear thus far that the reactions in School D are much more like those in the previous three schools than they are different in any way.

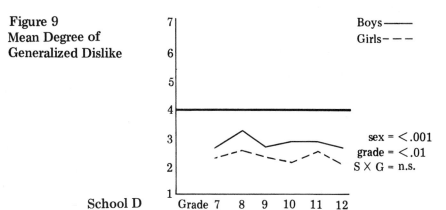

Figure 9
Mean Degree of
Generalized Dislike

School D

Conscientiousness

As in Schools A, B, and C, the girls are significantly more conscientious than the boys and the difference, especially in the upper grades, is large enough to be important (see figure 10). Again, there is a drop in conscientiousness as the students move up through the grades. The drop for boys is probably large enough to be taken seriously. It may reflect the sort of "pose" that happens at the college level, where it is not quite the thing to be a "greasy grind," and students who receive high marks rather often protest that they did not "do a bit of work." In this possible bit of role-playing there is a sex difference, just as in the data found here, for it is socially acceptable for a girl to be conscientious about her studies. And the S x G interaction is significant here, evidently because the downward trend for boys is clearer and stronger than that for girls. (If the data of the boys whose papers were discarded were in fact available, they would in all likelihood lower the means for conscientiousness; for me it is hard to believe otherwise.)

Anxiety and guilt about school

As shown in figure 11 and as might be expected, the girls are significantly higher on these ratings than are the boys. There is

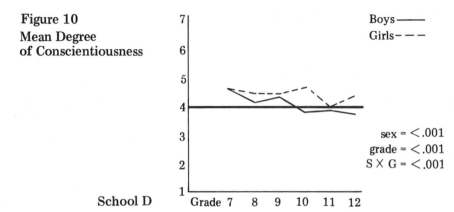

Figure 10
Mean Degree
of Conscientiousness

Boys ——
Girls – – –

sex = <.001
grade = <.001
S X G = <.001

School D   Grade 7   8   9   10   11   12

also a significant decrease across the grades, as in the other three
schools. Since the trend is comparable between the sexes, the
S x G interaction is insignificant.

Here is another confirmation of higher than neutral self-ratings
of anxiety and guilt among the boys in grades 7, 8, and 9 and
confirmation also of the decrease in anxiety and guilt ratings
among girls as they move toward senior year. Insofar as the actual
mean ratings are concerned, School D is probably as low in anxiety-guilt as any other school studied. This does not deter me
from my concern that enough students have such feelings that
the mean ratings are as high as they are. It does not suffice, I
think, merely to say that adolescence is an anxious period of life.

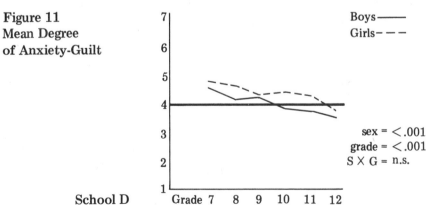

Figure 11
Mean Degree
of Anxiety-Guilt

Boys ——
Girls – – –

sex = <.001
grade = <.001
S X G = n.s.

School D   Grade 7   8   9   10   11   12

Favorable attitude toward teachers

We see in figure 12 that the students in School D tend to like teachers. The girls' ratings are significantly stronger than the boys' (although the boys' ratings, as in all other schools studied, are definitely above the neutral level), and there is a significant increase in this favorable attitude the higher the grade level of the student. The latter finding is statistically clear, but the trend is probably not consistent enough to be impressive. The S x G interaction is insignificant. Within the limits already referred to with respect to comparisons of schools, School D in general produces the same kinds of attitudes toward teachers, but the degree of favorableness may be slightly less here. If that is indeed so, I have no explanation for it.

Figure 12
Mean Degree of
Liking for Teachers

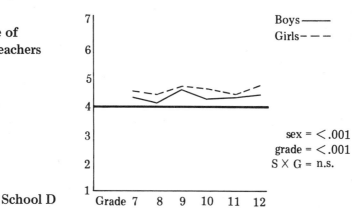

School D

sex = < .001
grade = < .001
S X G = n.s.

Social distractibility

Again we find no evidence that girls are more distractible than boys (see figure 13). We do find a significant variation across grades, however, and interestingly enough, a significant S x G interaction. Taking the two latter statements together, we see in figure 13 that girls rate themselves as less distractible than boys in the seventh grade, equally so in the eighth grade, and more so in all grades except the twelfth, where they drop well below the boys. The significant across-grades effect and the significant interaction occurred previously only in School C, and there the pattern of variation was different. I am therefore inclined to say we do not

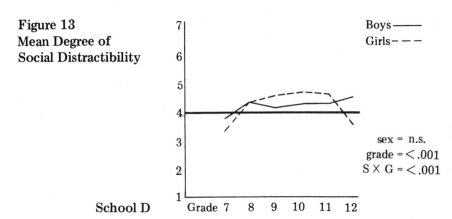

Figure 13
Mean Degree of
Social Distractibility

Boys ——
Girls – – –

sex = n.s.
grade = <.001
S X G = <.001

School D   Grade 7   8   9   10   11   12

know what variations to expect, and, obviously, any of these
curves may be reflecting something about conditions in a particular school or community. Nonetheless, it would appear that
School D, on this scale as on others, produces results more similar to those previously reported than different.

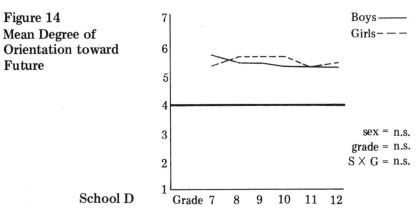

Figure 14
Mean Degree of
Orientation toward
Future

Boys ——
Girls – – –

sex = n.s.
grade = n.s.
S X G = n.s.

School D   Grade 7   8   9   10   11   12

Orientation toward the future

As in every other school, this scale produced the highest means
of all (see figure 14). None of the comparisons made produced a
significant result, for both sexes in all the grades rated themselves
about the same. There is a visual impression that boys drift downward in degree of concern from seventh grade, whereas girls re-

main fairly steady; the statistical evaluation of S x G, however, simply does not reach a significant level. The means shown here are perhaps .2 to .4 of a scale step lower than in the other systems, but as is shown, they are nevertheless high. So it again seems reasonable that School D is comparable to the others.

The New Scale

Giving a special heading to a discussion of the new scale somehow makes it seem more important than the first seven. This is not the case, and the special heading is intended merely to set this discussion apart from what has gone before because this study was done especially to discover whether the scale purporting to measure favorable attitude toward the school as a social system seems to make more complete or analytical the descriptions previously provided by the first seven scales. I have already noted that it was not possible to replicate the use of this particular scale, and I can feel justified in discussing it only by assuming that if the first seven scales produce results in School D that are a reasonable replication of results secured elsewhere, the new scale likewise will produce results that will be replicable elsewhere in the future. The data concerning intensity and direction of attitude are shown in figure 15. Exact values are recorded in appendix I.

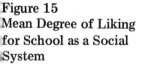

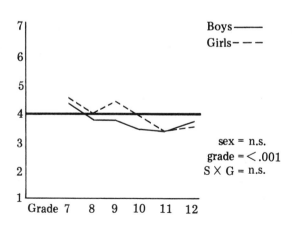

Figure 15
Mean Degree of Liking
for School as a Social
System

Boys ———
Girls – – –

sex = n.s.
grade = < .001
S × G = n.s.

School D   Grade 7   8   9   10   11   12

Perhaps the first thing to note is that the sexes do not differ significantly. The variation across grades is statistically very significant and would appear to be large enough to deserve serious attention. Especially in grades 10, 11, and 12 both boys and girls rate the school as a social system unfavorably, on the average. Since both sexes in the seventh grade give a somewhat favorable rating to the system, but both tend to give lower ratings thereafter, the S x G interaction is insignificant. There is no clear indication here that the group I have come to think of as the "angry young men" would have changed the results, but I had a firm impression while I was examining their papers before discarding them that what they wrote signified that many of them, if their remarks were to be taken literally, hated the system as a system and said so flatly.

It seems desirable in this particular case to examine the data for individual statements. I therefore record each statement, indicate whether answers to it were reversed numerically in scoring, and show the median rounded to the nearest whole scale step for boys and girls separately in grades 10, 11, and 12 (columns 1, 2, and 3). (To repeat, a high score means a very favorable attitude toward the school as a social system.)

1. More freedom to make my own decisions in school would be very important to me. (Scoring reversed)

Boys	3.0	2.0	3.0
Girls	3.0	2.0	3.0

18. Our principal treats us as though we're just things, not real people. (Reversed)

Boys	4.0	4.0	4.0
Girls	4.0	4.0	3.0

22. I think that except for a few requirements, the school should relax and let us learn what we want to learn, when we want to learn it. (Reversed)

Boys	3.0	3.0	3.0
Girls	4.0	3.0	3.0

36. I think the school has to have strict control of students in order to know who's doing what, where and when.

Boys	3.0	2.0	3.0
Girls	4.0	2.0	2.0

42. I feel schools have to have a lot of rules just to operate.

Boys	3.0	3.0	3.0
Girls	3.0	3.0	3.0

47. I think students are treated too much alike in school, even though we all know each is different from the others. (Reversed)

Boys	3.0	3.0	3.0
Girls	3.0	3.0	4.0

56. I like learning but I *don't* like school. (Reversed)

Boys	4.0	3.0	4.0
Girls	4.0	3.0	4.0

59. Even though someone else decides on them, I think the subjects we study here are the best ones for a good education.

Boys	4.0	3.0	4.0
Girls	4.0	4.0	4.0

74. I object strongly to having to have signed passes for every unusual thing we do. (Reversed)

Boys	2.0	1.0	2.0
Girls	2.0	1.0	2.0

85. Having a regular schedule of classes makes me feel secure about what's coming next.

Boys	4.0	4.0	3.0
Girls	3.0	3.0	3.0

Thus we see that on a scale where 7 would mean a very favorable attitude toward the school as a social system, no median is above 4.0 (neutrality), and 41 out of 60 are below that. This occurs despite the fact that numbers 56, 59, and 18 are statements evidently not tapping the "core" attitude very closely, in view of the number of medians at 4.0. Two of the statements are, in hindsight, not very good ones, despite their surviving the item analysis. No. 18 doesn't fit well in School D, where there are so many assistant principals that there is no way of designating which one is meant without using wording which makes the principal an overemphasized component of the system. No. 56 is double-barreled, i.e., one part can seem true, the other untrue, and such statements can produce legitimate "don't know" ratings by students.

Despite these probable shortcomings of the scale, we can feel confident that certain of the statements tap very strong attitudes

among many students: they do not like being treated alike; they
come close to despising the pass system; they would like more
choice about what to study and when to study it; they think
there are too many rules; they would like more decision-making
power; they do not feel the school has to have such strict controls;
and they are rather against schedules.

For how long students have felt this way I wouldn't know. Such
feelings played a considerable part in the uprisings in the colleges
of the nation a few years ago and since, and have been implicit
in many of the disorders in schools—discernible apart from race
problems, as we may infer from the opinions of authors such as
Silberman (1970, esp. chap. 8). Silberman speaks of adolescents
as being "harder to control" than younger children, and the reactions of the students as reported here suggest that the school
has responded by developing restrictive and controlling measures
or devices.

The Patterning of Attitudes in School D

In chapter 8 an analysis was made of attitude patterns in
Schools A, B, and C, following upon a chapter concerned with
intensity and direction of attitudes. In this chapter we are dealing directly with one school only, and so it seems appropriate to
include the pattern analysis here. Because we are now reporting
on eight scales rather than seven, I shall use one- or two-letter
abbreviations to save space in indicating which scale is which in
table 4. The abbreviations are: L = positive and active liking for
school; D = generalized dislike of school; C = conscientiousness;
A = anxiety and guilt about school; T = favorable attitude toward
teachers; So = social distractibility; F = orientation toward the
future; and Sy = favorable attitude toward the school as a social
system. Table 4, for ease of reporting and discussion, shows only
rs which are averages across the six grades (see appendix J for
breakdown into grades).

With respect to the first seven scales, comparison with tables 2
and 3 suggests that, in general, the scales intercorrelate in School
D as they did in earlier schools, and that the sexes yield very
similar results. The rs again fall into two patterns of scales. The
first and larger one includes liking for school, conscientiousness,

Table 4. Intercorrelations of the Eight Scales Used in School D

	Sex	D	C	A	T	So	F	Sy
L	M	-.34	.57	.23	.39	-.29	.31	.27
	F	-.41	.62	.17	.40	-.37	.36	.32
D	M		-.49	-.08	-.52	.50	-.46	-.51
	F		-.50	-.11	-.56	.47	-.53	-.52
C	M			.33	.37	-.43	.35	.38
	F			.35	.42	-.45	.43	.46
A	M				.09	-.06	.20	.13
	F				.11	.01	.19	.20
T	M					-.33	.36	.53
	F					-.36	.46	.55
So	M						-.18	-.32
	F						-.21	-.32
F	M							.35
	F							.45

Sex	n	p=<.01
M	1006	.08
F	1061	.08

liking for teachers, and concern for the future. The smaller pattern contains just two scales: dislike and social distractibility. (Remember that the definition of a pattern is that scales within it correlate positively with each other and poorly or negatively with all other scales.) As before, anxiety and guilt feelings cannot be placed with confidence in either pattern. Note that in this school the anxiety-guilt scale correlates rather well with conscientiousness, which in theory it should. It also correlates positively with liking for school, which at least is plausible on the assumption that those who like school are also concerned about it and would, for example, dislike or fear failing there. But anxiety-guilt correlates hardly at all with liking for teachers, which is in the same pattern with liking for school and conscientiousness, and even less closely with social distractibility or dislike of school, which form the other pattern. And, more confusing still, anxiety-guilt correlates positively with concern for the future, which I tend to place in the large pattern of attitudes. I therefore have the feeling, in School D as elsewhere, that anxiety-guilt cannot surely be placed in either of the identifiable patterns.

Now let us see how the scale purporting to measure favorableness of attitude toward the school as a social system relates to the other scales. The last column of table 4 shows that almost without question this scale belongs to the first-named or large pattern of scales. It correlates positively with liking for school, negatively with dislike for school, and so on down the line. The ambiguous *r*s, again, are with anxiety-guilt, for on the surface of it, a positive *r* does not seem very plausible here. Since all the other *r*s with attitude toward the system seem to drop into place, I should prefer for the present to say there is insufficient information to place anxiety-guilt in a pattern.

Perhaps it should go without saying, but I remind you that the foregoing analysis of intercorrelations of scales is, in fact, an analysis of the patterning of attitudes in a small area of a person's complex make-up. That is, we have been talking about that aspect of personality make-up or structure which, in the students discussed here, has to do with their predispositions to react in certain ways to certain aspects of school or schooling. This leads me to a final report on an aspect of appendix J which is not shown here, but about which I have remarked in other schools. This has to do with personality individuation, as shown by a decreasing size of *r*s among scales as students move through adolescence. As in the tables of *r*s from previous schools, I tallied the number of times, for a given scale, that the twelfth grade *r* was smaller than the seventh grade *r* or showed some other result. In School D the results are very clear for girls (24 decreases versus 4 other, chi-square significant at <.01), but not so clear for boys (18 decreases versus 10 other). It may be remembered that in School B there was an insignificant result from this kind of tally for both sexes. Now in School D, a comparable school, girls show a significant change but boys show only a trend. (If the same test is made omitting the correlations of other scales with that concerned with the school as a system, exactly the same results are found.) I therefore continue to feel that individuation is going on, even according to the insensitive test I have used, and the fact that it is clearer in girls than in boys is merely an aspect of the earlier development of girls. In so saying,

I continue to disregard the results from School B but by implication take into account the findings for girls in School D.

This rather rapid review of the data from School D has achieved two principal goals. First, it has shown that in still a fourth school system, approximately the same results occur with respect to the intensity and direction of attitudes, as well as in the patterning of attitudes shown by intercorrelations of scales. These statements, of course, are made cautiously because the questionnaire was somewhat modified. At any rate, it is assumed that School D is not likely to yield drastically atypical information on the new scale which this second study was intended to develop and use. The second goal was fairly well reached. The new scale suggests that particularly the older students (grades 10, 11, and 12) do not like the school very much as a social system.

The organization of this book is such that Part 1 presents the rationale for the studies, the opinions arrived at after an evaluation of my own data, and supplementation by other data or widely accepted opinion which were woven into the discussion of the way the adolescent fits the school and vice versa. Part 2 is a rather straightforward report on my own work, and it is necessary therefore only to summarize it with a few additional comments about the meaning of the results.

What's new in these pages is the report of *measured* attitudes of students toward school. These data were collected systematically in a manner which attempts to assure truthful expression and avoid sampling biases. In fact, the students are not a sample, except in the sense that all students in grades 7 through 12 who came to school in a certain town on a certain day constitute a sample. They expressed themselves by answering a questionnaire rather than by discussing their attitudes in an interview, thus avoiding the nuances arising in the relationship of interviewer to the person interviewed. This is hardly to say that the anonymous questionnaire is without its own problems, but at least we have recorded the reactions of 6,500 consumers of education (the round number is sheer coincidence) in four different school systems. We are now able to summarize, for the first time, the high points of all that has been recorded previously in this study. We can then indicate where the reactions of students to school seem to run counter to what we might hope would be their situation in school. Despite the fact that the data are descriptive only, it seems reasonable to yield occasionally to the temptation to speculate on why certain findings appear.

Intensities and directions of attitudes: similarities and differences

Anyone who has read this far will have been impressed, I think, with the fact that although the school systems in which data were collected were deliberately selected to be quite different

from one another along a "quality" dimension, the results of
measuring a variety of attitudes toward school yield impressively
similar results for each attitude and some rather discouraging
ones, despite some significant variations among communities,
sexes, grades, and interactions among various of these.

1. Students, on the whole, are indifferent to school. The
younger students (grade 7 mainly, but one grade 8 and one grade
9 subgroup also) show a little liking for school but older students
tend to show lower averages. Although in 7 of 8 comparisons
(2 sexes, 4 schools) there is a slight increase among juniors and/
or seniors, the curves for both sexes in all four schools remain
about at the indifference level. This finding is probably akin to
that of Donaghy (1970, pp. 1070-71), who found that personality factors, and to a lesser extent such things as conflict with
parents, were associated with the fact that certain students differed from others in attitude toward school; this led Donaghy to
the comment that students seem to take an attitude of "practical"
acceptance toward school.

2. Just as clearly, in all four schools the students on the average deny disliking school. Girls deny more strongly than boys in
all four schools, and the denial is rather inconsistently greater
among more advanced students, as measured by a scale contain-
ing quite different statements from the liking scale. This raises
our first question: Is the firm and consistent denial of dislike
simply an affirmation of indifference to school or does it mean
something else? I have suggested, then disparaged, the possibility
that response set was significantly involved in these data, i.e., that
students, even in anonymity, did not want to rate a number of
rather unflattering statements as being very true of them. But it
is not possible to rule out the possibility that on the average the
students are so indifferent to school that it would be incorrect
for them to say they disliked it.

3. Girls everywhere are more conscientious on the average than
boys, although usually the mean rating for boys is also on the
side of conscientiousness, and there is a statistically significant
and perhaps practically important decrease in conscientiousness
among more advanced students. In the three-school study there
was some tendency for conscientiousness to be greatest in the
most favored (or highest quality) school, lower in the middle

school, and lowest in the least favored school. This tendency is made less clear by the fourth school, which I described as being in the middle in quality in several respects but seemingly closer to the most favored school in certain respects; conscientiousness tends to be lower here than in any other school reported.

So we extend the problem posed above: not only are students apathetic about school and unwilling to deny firmly that they dislike it, but they assert quite clearly in three out of four schools (and among girls and younger boys in the fourth school) that they are conscientious about school. So here we have it: their attitudes toward school are seemingly inconsistent, and it is difficult to avoid speculating that this influences the way they conduct themselves in school. One can also add the speculation that they are indeed conscientious, and this is a generalized trait that keeps them at their schoolwork despite their indifference toward it.

4. Everywhere, on the average, girls are more willing to admit to feelings of anxiety and guilt about school than are boys. For boys in all schools the rating of anxiety is above 4.0 in grades 7, 8, and 9, but drops below 4.0 in grade 10 or 11. For girls the decrease is also evident, starting from a higher level than for boys in grade 7 and dropping below 4.0: not at all in School A; only once in what looks like a fluke in grade 11 girls in School B; by .1 scale step in grade 12 in School C; and by .2 scale step in grade 12, School D. In other words, it is not convincingly clear that girls at any grade level rate themselves at less than indifference on this scale. There were significant school differences (Schools C and D being a little lower than A and B in most comparisons), but the variation does not seem importantly large. One nevertheless must deplore the anxiety present in so many.

5. On the whole, teachers are liked in every school, more by girls than by boys, and rather unclearly so by the more advanced students (this was significantly so in Schools C and D, but not in Schools A and B). As I said before, this general attitude was somewhat surprising to me. It nevertheless now suggests that teachers may be a positive resource for change.

6. Social distractibility (here defined as negative in its effect) was evident in means above 4.0 in two thirds or more of all subgroups in Schools B, C, and D, and in all subgroups in School A.

The only sex difference occurred in School C, where the boys were less distractible than the girls. In two schools (C and D) there was a significant but only moderately large interaction of grade and sex, but the interactions took quite different forms in the schools, so we are only able to say that they are different. (This statement should perhaps have been made specific previously, for one of the notable observations one makes, in the search for generalizations about schools, is the intangible yet somehow very real fact that the atmosphere, if I may call it that, can seem to change as quickly as one can leave one building and enter another, even within the same school system. I am inclined to attribute much, but not all, of this variation to the administration within a given building.)

7. Concern for the relation of schooling to the future was high everywhere. This was such a dominating aspect of the data that the significant differences between the sexes (Schools A and B) and across the grades (Schools A, C, and D) are not as noticeable as they otherwise might be. One can easily speculate that this concern, which I called instrumental, is related to the fact that students stay in school even though they are indifferent toward it. It is typical for a student to believe that schooling can make a difference in his future.

8. Only in School D was the scale measuring favorable attitude toward the school as a social system used. (Since in all other aspects School D seemed to yield results strongly resembling those in the three-school study, it is hoped that a sort of reverse assumption will turn out to be correct: results on this new scale in School D will prove to be replicable in other schools also.) The data for this scale showed that all means in grades higher than the seventh were below 4.0, notably so in grades 10, 11, and 12 for boys. For girls only the means for grades 11 and 12 (and to a lesser extent 10) were notably below 4.0. The sex difference is quite insignificant, and as the above remarks suggest, the variation for grades was sizable as well as significant. It is probably important.

The patterning of attitudes

The word *pattern* may be defined in several ways when one is working with statistical material, as has been said previously. Not to confuse this discussion by mentioning alternatives which would

not fit our situation very well, I have simply declared that by
pattern I mean any group of attitudes which correlate positively
with each other and either negatively or insignificantly with
other attitudes measured by the eight scales used here. A very
early comment about restriction of range should perhaps be repeated: because a student could choose only from among seven
possible indications (scale steps) as to how strongly he felt about
a particular statement, the correlations I discuss here are probably not as precise as they would be had the student been able
to give a more discriminating answer; I cannot tell whether the
more precise correlation would be higher or lower, so I shall
treat the correlations as the best available estimates of true
correlations.

   1. In the three-school study it appeared that the rs of the seven
scales fell out into two patterns, plus a scale which could not be
placed. The first and larger pattern of attitudes included those
called positive and active liking for school, conscientiousness,
liking for teachers, and orientation toward the future. The second
included generalized dislike for school and social distractibility.
(This suggests that degree of dislike for school and degree of
liking are indeed two different variables.) Anxiety and guilt feelings about school showed some signs of belonging in each group,
but there were also rs indicating that it did not really belong in
either. It was therefore not included in either, and indeed it was
suggested that further study may show that this factor either
stands alone or is part of some as yet unmeasured cluster of
attitudes.

   2. When School D was added in order to develop and employ
the eighth scale measuring attitude toward the school as a social
system, the two patterns of attitudes and the ambiguity appeared
to be the same as for the first seven scales. In addition, attitude
toward the school as a social system quite clearly must be added
to the first and larger pattern of attitudes. The second pattern
remains the same, and the anxiety-guilt scale again stands by itself, with small and inconsistent rs with all other attitudes
measured in these studies to date.

   The findings about adolescent attitude intensity, direction, and
pattern just summarized were what led me to the kinds of inter-

pretation and even extrapolation which give to Part 1 of this book the sober, concerned tone it has. I have taken the position that what has determined the mismatch between adolescents and schools is to a large extent the unwillingness or incapability to adapt of the junior and senior high schools and the communities in which they serve. I have also come to feel that less than new "programs" or facilities, a massive change in attitudes of all persons concerned with the schools is necessary. Can we develop a strategy for rising to that challenge?

Please do not write your name on this paper!

To begin with

There are lots of opinions about what our students think of schoolwork. Most of these opinions come from newspaper writers, parents, or other adults. People don't often seem to ask the students themselves what they think. This is what I want to do, and I ask for your cooperation in answering my questions.

As you will soon see, this is *not* a test, and there are *no* right or wrong answers. Instead, I shall ask for your opinions or attitudes on a good many things. You have noticed that I do not want to know your name. No one in this school will see your answers. This guarantees that you can put down exactly what you think. That's all that interests me.

What you are to do

In this paper there is a long list of statements or sentences that someone *might* say about school or schoolwork. Some of them are repeated in different words. You are to mark each sentence to show whether, *for you personally*, what it says is true, untrue, or something in between.

For example a sentence might be, "I think studying is a terrible waste of time."

	Very true						Very untrue
	+3	+2	+1	0	-1	-2	-3

Now, is that true or untrue for you personally? Notice that beside the sentence there is a row of numbers going from +3 at one end, which means "very true," through zero, which means "in between" or "don't know," to -3, which means "very untrue." *You are to circle the number that tells just how true or untrue the sentence is for you.* Many people, but perhaps not all, would feel that the sentence about studying being a waste of time is untrue for them. So I would probably find that many of you would circle a

number somewhere on the "untrue" or minus side of zero.

Another example might be
"Good work in school helps you
later on."
Many students would probably
think that true. So most of you
would circle a number somewhere on the "true" or plus
side of zero; but some would
perhaps feel the opposite way
and circle a minus number.

Very						Very
true						untrue
+3	+2	+1	0	-1	-2	-3

How to do it

1. Circle one and only one number for each sentence. I cannot guess
how many you will call true or untrue because that depends altogether
on how you feel.
2. If you decide to change an answer, scratch it out so I will be sure to
notice the change.
3. So many kinds of opinions are stated here that sooner or later you will
need to use all the possible numbers to indicate how you feel.

Do not turn the page until we see whether anyone has any questions!

Circle the correct one

School_____   Grade_____   Male   Female   Your age____

| | Very
true | | | | | | Very
untrue |

1. Before I hand in a test I check it carefully to make sure I haven't left anything out.   +3 +2 +1 0 -1 -2 -3

2. I think there's no one you can depend on more than a close friend.   +3 +2 +1 0 -1 -2 -3

3. If I have questions about something I have read outside class, I always try to bring them up in class.   +3 +2 +1 0 -1 -2 -3

4. I admire a teacher who can really take hold of a class and get it to learn.   +3 +2 +1 0 -1 -2 -3

5. If I don't like an assignment or a discussion, I often groan to show how I feel.   +3 +2 +1 0 -1 -2 -3

6. If I am having trouble learning something, I'd rather ask a friend for help than go to the teacher or my parents.   +3 +2 +1 0 -1 -2 -3

7. After I take a test I worry until I find out how well I did.   +3 +2 +1 0 -1 -2 -3

8. I like to read school books carefully.   +3 +2 +1 0 -1 -2 -3

9. I just take each school day as it comes and don't think about what's ahead.   +3 +2 +1 0 -1 -2 -3

10. I think most teachers feel sympathetic toward students or they wouldn't be in the job.   +3 +2 +1 0 -1 -2 -3

11. I usually don't pay attention in class.   +3 +2 +1 0 -1 -2 -3

12. I think it's interesting to pull together all the different things I learn in one course or class.   +3 +2 +1 0 -1 -2 -3

	Very true						Very untrue

13. I think having a lot of friends is important to enjoying school. $\quad$ +3 +2 +1 0 -1 -2 -3

14. I often damage school property to show I don't like being there. $\quad$ +3 +2 +1 0 -1 -2 -3

15. If something happens to make me look foolish in school, I think about it for a long time afterwards. $\quad$ +3 +2 +1 0 -1 -2 -3

16. I very much enjoy learning new words. $\quad$ +3 +2 +1 0 -1 -2 -3

17. I soon let teachers know they had better leave me alone. $\quad$ +3 +2 +1 0 -1 -2 -3

18. I am careful to be prepared when I expect a class discussion. $\quad$ +3 +2 +1 0 -1 -2 -3

19. I have had nightmares about not being able to do something correctly in school. $\quad$ +3 +2 +1 0 -1 -2 -3

20. If I think assignments are too difficult, I complain to the teacher. $\quad$ +3 +2 +1 0 -1 -2 -3

21. I care a lot more about having a good time with my friends in class than doing schoolwork. $\quad$ +3 +2 +1 0 -1 -2 -3

22. I like to work hardest at my most difficult subjects. $\quad$ +3 +2 +1 0 -1 -2 -3

23. If a teacher asks me to do something in front of a class, I am always afraid I am going to make some silly mistakes. $\quad$ +3 +2 +1 0 -1 -2 -3

24. I think boys need to be well educated because their jobs or careers will require it. $\quad$ +3 +2 +1 0 -1 -2 -3

25. Teachers put too much emphasis on learning facts and not enough on what they mean, in my opinion. $\quad$ +3 +2 +1 0 -1 -2 -3

26. I get a lot out of classroom discussions. $\quad$ +3 +2 +1 0 -1 -2 -3

	Very true	Very untrue

27. The reason I learn is mostly to
    avoid trouble.   +3 +2 +1 0 -1 -2 -3

28. If for any reason I have to speak
    to the principal, I get nervous.   +3 +2 +1 0 -1 -2 -3

29. I like teachers who keep strict
    control of the classroom.   +3 +2 +1 0 -1 -2 -3

30. I want to go on learning the rest
    of my life.   +3 +2 +1 0 -1 -2 -3

31. I just don't care whether a teacher
    likes my work or not.   +3 +2 +1 0 -1 -2 -3

32. I feel that if you're always trying
    to beat other people's grades,
    you're not going to make many
    friends.   +3 +2 +1 0 -1 -2 -3

33. Some subjects interest me so much
    that I read a lot more about them
    than is required.   +3 +2 +1 0 -1 -2 -3

34. I stay away from teachers because
    they're so bossy.   +3 +2 +1 0 -1 -2 -3

35. I always expect to be more con-
    fused after a discussion than I was
    before.   +3 +2 +1 0 -1 -2 -3

36. I like to pay close attention to a
    teacher.   +3 +2 +1 0 -1 -2 -3

37. I never get bored in class.   +3 +2 +1 0 -1 -2 -3

38. I worry a lot about school, but I
    don't like to talk about it.   +3 +2 +1 0 -1 -2 -3

39. I very often pass notes or talk to
    friends in class.   +3 +2 +1 0 -1 -2 -3

40. I feel that my teachers know a
    lot more about their subject than
    I do, so they can teach me a great
    deal.   +3 +2 +1 0 -1 -2 -3

41. To me, sports are more important
    than schoolwork.   +3 +2 +1 0 -1 -2 -3

	Very true						Very untrue

42. I find that homework is almost always helpful in my learning. +3 +2 +1 0 -1 -2 -3

43. I think girls really don't need a lot of education, because they will probably just get married and raise a family. +3 +2 +1 0 -1 -2 -3

44. I like the social activities, such as clubs, far more than the other parts of school. +3 +2 +1 0 -1 -2 -3

45. I think the best teachers are friendly but at the same time take no nonsense from the class. +3 +2 +1 0 -1 -2 -3

46. The world is changing so fast that most of what we learn now isn't going to be worth much in the future. +3 +2 +1 0 -1 -2 -3

47. I think schools have a lot of senseless rules. +3 +2 +1 0 -1 -2 -3

48. I'm pretty sure what's going to happen to me in the next ten years, and I don't think schooling has much to do with it. +3 +2 +1 0 -1 -2 -3

49. I think it's important to plan my study time and my work. +3 +2 +1 0 -1 -2 -3

50. If a good friend of mine does something stupid in school, it makes me very unhappy. +3 +2 +1 0 -1 -2 -3

51. I have been good friends with several of my teachers at one time or another, and I continue to like them. +3 +2 +1 0 -1 -2 -3

52. I enjoy inventing or suggesting projects for work in school. +3 +2 +1 0 -1 -2 -3

53. I feel very ashamed if I do poor work. +3 +2 +1 0 -1 -2 -3

54. The people who quit school are some day going to be very sorry they did. +3 +2 +1 0 -1 -2 -3

	Very true					Very untrue

55. If a classroom discussion gets
confused, I feel I ought to help
get things straightened out.   +3 +2 +1 0 -1 -2 -3

56. I try hard to make my written
work neat and orderly.   +3 +2 +1 0 -1 -2 -3

57. I like school and I like learning.   +3 +2 +1 0 -1 -2 -3

58. I feel sympathetic with teachers
because they have to do so much
besides teaching.   +3 +2 +1 0 -1 -2 -3

59. I like to get together with one or
more friends to do homework.   +3 +2 +1 0 -1 -2 -3

60. To make sure I don't forget, I
frequently go back over earlier
lessons.   +3 +2 +1 0 -1 -2 -3

61. I am staying in school so I can
get into college.   +3 +2 +1 0 -1 -2 -3

62. About the only reason I come to
school is to see my friends.   +3 +2 +1 0 -1 -2 -3

63. If I see how to help a teacher plan
or do something better, I am quick
to suggest it.   +3 +2 +1 0 -1 -2 -3

64. A lot of teachers want to be
popular with students, so they
let the students get away with
just about anything.   +3 +2 +1 0 -1 -2 -3

65. The thought of failure makes
my hands perspire.   +3 +2 +1 0 -1 -2 -3

66. I often wish someone would tell
me why I have to go to school
anyway.   +3 +2 +1 0 -1 -2 -3

67. I always try to hand in my work
on time.   +3 +2 +1 0 -1 -2 -3

68. I think that if you don't keep
looking ahead to future life, you
won't get the most out of school.   +3 +2 +1 0 -1 -2 -3

69. I hate school.   +3 +2 +1 0 -1 -2 -3

	Very true	Very untrue

70. I really like clubs or activities connected with school subjects that interest me. +3 +2 +1 0 −1 −2 −3

71. I just don't like tests. +3 +2 +1 0 −1 −2 −3

72. Most of what I learn in school isn't going to help in my future life. +3 +2 +1 0 −1 −2 −3

73. Several times I have thought I wouldn't like a class, but the teacher changed my mind. +3 +2 +1 0 −1 −2 −3

74. If a lesson is difficult for me, I'd rather daydream than work at it. +3 +2 +1 0 −1 −2 −3

75. I like to have the same classes as my friends. +3 +2 +1 0 −1 −2 −3

76. If I know I am to be absent from school, I like to get my class assignments in advance. +3 +2 +1 0 −1 −2 −3

77. When a teacher says we are going to be given a test, my heart begins to beat faster. +3 +2 +1 0 −1 −2 −3

78. It seems to me that many of my teachers are overly quick to be suspicious of a student. +3 +2 +1 0 −1 −2 −3

79. I like to go to or from school with the same group of people. +3 +2 +1 0 1 2 −3

80. I think students really ought to stick with something until they finish it. +3 +2 +1 0 −1 −2 −3

81. I think the high school diploma is a necessary "ticket of admission" to many jobs and all colleges. +3 +2 +1 0 −1 −2 −3

82. I worry about what my classmates think of me. +3 +2 +1 0 −1 −2 −3

	Very true						Very untrue

83. If I have to choose between
spending time with a friend and
getting something done for school,
the friend always wins.   +3 +2 +1 0 −1 −2 −3

84. I like very much to be with good
students.   +3 +2 +1 0 −1 −2 −3

85. I am very concerned about the
quality of my schoolwork, and
so I try to figure out my strong
and weak points.   +3 +2 +1 0 −1 −2 −3

86. I think I could do better on tests
if I could just stop worrying
about them.   +3 +2 +1 0 −1 −2 −3

87. I think going to school is just
about absolutely necessary for
getting along in the world today.   +3 +2 +1 0 −1 −2 −3

88. Praise from a teacher is important
to me.   +3 +2 +1 0 −1 −2 −3

89. I certainly think you should
try for good grades in all subjects, even though some of them
don't interest you.   +3 +2 +1 0 −1 −2 −3

90. My mind often wanders when I
am trying to study.   +3 +2 +1 0 −1 −2 −3

91. It feels good to understand some-
thing fully.   +3 +2 +1 0 −1 −2 −3

92. I am going to quit school just as
soon as I can, so I can get a job.   +3 +2 +1 0 −1 −2 −3

93. Sometimes when I don't understand something I feel I really
must be dumb.   +3 +2 +1 0 −1 −2 −3

94. Most teachers are too old to
understand the problems or in-
terests of students.   +3 +2 +1 0 −1 −2 −3

95. I feel bad if I get a much higher
grade than a good friend.   +3 +2 +1 0 −1 −2 −3

	Very true						Very untrue

96. I think the better educated you are, the better life you can lead in the future.   +3 +2 +1 0 −1 −2 −3

97. I very much like to help the teacher with classroom chores, such as moving furniture, giving out papers, or cleaning the board.   +3 +2 +1 0 −1 −2 −3

98. Because I'm afraid I might not finish on time, I quite often work too fast and make mistakes.   +3 +2 +1 0 −1 −2 −3

Positive and active liking for school

3. If I have questions about something I have read outside class, I always try to bring them up in class.
12. I think it's interesting to pull together all the different things I learn in one course or class.
16. I very much enjoy learning new words.
26. I get a lot out of classroom discussions.
33. Some subjects interest me so much that I read a lot more about them than is required.
37. I never get bored in class.
52. I enjoy inventing or suggesting projects for work in school.
55. If a classroom discussion gets confused, I feel I ought to help get things straightened out.
57. I like school and I like learning.
63. If I see how to help a teacher plan or do something better, I am quick to suggest it.
70. I really like clubs or activities connected with school subjects that interest me.
84. I like very much to be with good students.
91. It feels good to understand something fully.
97. I very much like to help the teacher with classroom chores, such as moving furniture, giving out papers, or cleaning the board.

Generalized dislike of school

5. If I don't like an assignment or a discussion, I often groan to show how I feel.
11. I usually don't pay attention in class.
14. I often damage school property to show I don't like being there.
17. I soon let teachers know they had better leave me alone.
20. If I think assignments are too difficult, I complain to the teacher.
27. The reason I learn is mostly to avoid trouble.
31. I just don't care whether a teacher likes my work or not.
35. I always expect to be more confused after a discussion than I was before.
41. To me, sports are more important than schoolwork.
47. I think schools have a lot of senseless rules.
66. I often wish someone would tell me why I have to go to school anyway.
69. I hate school.
74. If a lesson is difficult for me, I'd rather daydream than work at it.

Conscientiousness

1. Before I hand in a test I check it carefully to make sure I haven't left anything out.
8. I like to read school books carefully.
18. I am careful to be prepared when I expect a class discussion.
22. I like to work hardest at my most difficult subjects.
36. I like to pay close attention to a teacher.
42. I find that homework is almost always helpful in my learning.
49. I think it's important to plan my study time and my work.
56. I try hard to make my written work neat and orderly.
60. To make sure I don't forget, I frequently go back over earlier lessons.
67. I always try to hand in my work on time.
76. If I know I am to be absent from school, I like to get my class assignments in advance.
80. I think students really ought to stick with something until they finish it.
85. I am very concerned about the quality of my schoolwork, and so I try to figure out my strong and weak points.
89. I certainly think you should try for good grades in all subjects, even though some of them don't interest you.

Anxiety and guilt about school

7. After I take a test I worry until I find out how well I did.
15. If something happens to make me look foolish in school, I think about it for a long time afterwards.
19. I have had nightmares about not being able to do something correctly in school.
23. If a teacher asks me to do something in front of a class, I am always afraid I am going to make some silly mistakes.
28. If for any reason I have to speak to the principal, I get nervous.
38. I worry a lot about school, but I don't like to talk about it.
53. I feel very ashamed if I do poor work.
65. The thought of failure makes my hands perspire.
77. When a teacher says we are going to be given a test, my heart begins to beat faster.
82. I worry about what my classmates think of me.
86. I think I could do better on tests if I could just stop worrying about them.
93. Sometimes when I don't understand something I feel I really must be dumb.
98. Because I'm afraid I might not finish on time, I quite often work too fast and make mistakes.

Favorable attitude toward teachers

  4. I admire a teacher who can really take hold of a class and get it to learn.

25. Teachers put too much emphasis on learning facts and not enough on what they mean, in my opinion.

29. I like teachers who keep strict control of the classroom.

*R 34. I stay away from teachers because they're so bossy.

40. I feel that my teachers know a lot more about their subject than I do, so they can teach me a great deal.

45. I think the best teachers are friendly but at the same time take no nonsense from the class.

51. I have been good friends with several of my teachers at one time or another, and I continue to like them.

58. I feel sympathetic with teachers because they have to do so much besides teaching.

R 78. It seems to me that many of my teachers are overly quick to be suspicious of a student.

88. Praise from a teacher is important to me.

R 94. Most teachers are too old to understand the problems or interests of students.

Social distractibility

  2. I think there's no one you can depend on more than a close friend.

  6. If I am having trouble learning something, I'd rather ask a friend for help than go to the teacher or my parents.

13. I think having a lot of friends is important to enjoying school.

21. I care a lot more about having a good time with my friends in class than doing schoolwork.

32. I feel that if you're always trying to beat other people's grades, you're not going to make many friends.

39. I very often pass notes or talk to friends in class.

44. I like the social activities, such as clubs, far more than the other parts of school.

62. About the only reason I come to school is to see my friends.

75. I like to have the same classes as my friends.

79. I like to go to or from school with the same group of people.

83. If I have to choose between spending time with a friend and getting something done for school, the friend always wins.

Orientation toward the future

R 9. I just take each school day as it comes and don't think about what's ahead.

*"R" means that the scoring for the statement was reversed, as explained on page 43.

30. I want to go on learning the rest of my life.
R 43. I think girls really don't need a lot of education because they will probably just get married and raise a family.
R 46. The world is changing so fast that most of what we learn now isn't going to be worth much in the future.
R 48. I'm pretty sure what's going to happen to me in the next ten years, and I don't think schooling has much to do with it.
54. The people who quit school are some day going to be very sorry they did.
61. I am staying in school so I can get into college.
68. I think that if you don't keep looking ahead to future life, you won't get the most out of school.
R 72. Most of what I learn in school isn't going to help in my future life.
81. I think the high school diploma is a necessary "ticket of admission" to many jobs and all colleges.
87. I think going to school is just about absolutely necessary for getting along in the world today.
R 92. I am going to quit school just as soon as I can, so I can get a job.
96. I think the better educated you are, the better life you can lead in the future.

APPENDIX C:
Reliability Coefficients in Schools A, B, and C

	Positive and active liking			Generalized dislike			Conscientiousness			Anxiety-guilt			Liking for teachers			Social distractibility			Orientation toward future		
	A	B	C	A	B	C	A	B	C	A	B	C	A	B	C	A	B	C	A	B	C
Boys Grade																					
7	.74	.58	.74	.72	.70	.79	.72	.73	.71	.70	.74	.71	.58	.59	.66	.57	.57	.60	.72	.75	.62
8	.76	.77	.63	.75	.61	.74	.78	.80	.76	.70	.67	.72	.38	.75	.62	.64	.63	.74	.62	.69	.80
9	.78	.79	.76	.70	.76	.73	.81	.64	.84	.56	.61	.69	.60	.73	.61	.45	.60	.85	.70	.61	.83
10	.71	.73	.67	.70	.51	.58	.80	.68	.77	.69	.63	.61	.58	.53	.55	.62	.37	.54	.70	.58	.79
11	.74	.69	.62	.74	.64	.64	.81	.69	.75	.80	.52	.63	.31	.53	.62	.43	.36	.61	.75	.62	.77
12	.59	.87	.68	.61	.56	.80	.56	.77	.76	.66	.74	.70	.66	.57	.48	.80	.63	.58	.59	.45	.56
Girls Grade																					
7	.79	.76	.81	.54	.69	.72	.73	.66	.75	.62	.56	.71	.60	.48	.58	.59	.56	.61	.75	.70	.68
8	.83	.72	.72	.72	.72	.71	.81	.64	.67	.55	.76	.76	.70	.59	.52	.57	.77	.55	.75	.69	.70
9	.73	.84	.77	.73	.78	.70	.70	.60	.58	.72	.59	.67	.58	.61	.63	.55	.65	.71	.79	.51	.71
10	.70	.84	.61	.66	.76	.62	.63	.84	.74	.61	.78	.27	.62	.66	.45	.65	.45	.61	.58	.76	.51
11	.79	.78	.67	.72	.59	.44	.64	.53	.78	.72	.66	.70	.54	.44	.63	.50	.70	.60	.64	.63	.66
12	.71	.76	.61	.61	.75	.40	.73	.80	.78	.76	.69	.76	.60	.39	.41	.53	.64	.45	.50	.74	.65
High	.83	.87	.81	.74	.78	.80	.81	.84	.84	.80	.76	.76	.70	.75	.66	.80	.77	.85	.79	.76	.83
Low	.59	.58	.61	.54	.56	.40	.56	.53	.58	.55	.52	.27	.31	.39	.41	.43	.36	.45	.50	.45	.51
Mean	.74	.76	.69	.68	.67	.66	.73	.70	.74	.67	.66	.66	.56	.57	.56	.58	.58	.62	.67	.64	.69
Grand mean	.73			.67			.72			.66			.56			.59			.67		

All of the analyses of variance reported here for the separate scales for Schools A, B, and C were based on a least-squares model because it was not initially intended to make inclusive statistical comparisons of the three schools and because the ns in different cells were so different it was thought that nonadditivity might be a problem. Later, when it seemed desirable to make the across-schools analysis, we shifted to a regression model with a program enabling us to determine degree of nonadditivity and learned that this model was very suitable.

This means that the last analysis presented for each scale in appendix D is based on the regression model, whereas the initial analyses are based on a least-squares model. (In the computer program used for the regression model the highest-order interaction was included in the residual.)

Scale 1: Positive and Active Liking for School

		School A			School B			School C		
Boys		m	SD	n	m	SD	n	m	SD	n
Grade	7	4.3	1.7	149	4.3	1.6	112	4.6	1.5	130
	8	4.3	1.6	148	4.0	1.6	111	4.3	1.4	127
	9	3.7	1.6	165	4.0	1.6	76	4.1	1.5	135
	10	3.9	1.6	160	3.7	1.5	57	4.0	1.3	138
	11	3.8	1.6	117	4.3	1.4	57	3.8	1.3	150
	12	4.1	1.3	104	4.0	1.5	64	4.1	1.3	146
Girls										
Grade	7	4.5	1.8	184	4.3	1.6	124	4.3	1.5	147
	8	4.1	1.8	179	4.0	1.5	88	4.1	1.6	136
	9	3.9	1.7	139	4.3	1.7	80	3.9	1.5	142
	10	3.9	1.7	180	4.2	1.7	82	4.0	1.3	133
	11	4.0	1.6	168	3.8	1.6	59	3.9	1.4	152
	12	4.1	1.5	126	4.4	1.6	58	4.3	1.3	110
Total ns				1819			968			1646

	Sex	Grade	S x G	Sex	Grade	S x G	Sex	Grade	S x G
F	<1.0	6.61	<1.0	<1.0	1.34	1.67	1.42	5.24	1.14
df	1/1807	5/1807	5/1807	1/956	5/956	5/956	1/1634	5/1634	5/1634
p	—	<.001	—	—	—	—	—	<.001	—

	F	df	p
Schools (Sc)	<1.0	2/4406	—
Sexes (S)	<1.0	1/4406	—
Grades (G)	10.00	5/4406	<.001
Sc x S	1.47	2/4406	—
Sc x G	1.13	10/4406	—
S x G	<1.0	5/4406	—
Correction for mean		1	

Scale 2: Generalized Dislike of School

	School A			School B			School C		
Boys	m	SD	n	m	SD	n	m	SD	n
Grade 7	3.0	1.8	149	2.8	1.6	112	2.7	1.6	130
8	3.1	1.8	148	2.8	1.6	111	2.7	1.6	127
9	3.4	1.7	165	2.9	1.5	76	2.9	1.5	135
10	2.8	1.5	160	3.0	1.4	57	2.4	1.1	138
11	3.4	1.8	117	2.6	1.3	57	2.5	1.3	150
12	2.8	1.4	104	2.7	1.5	64	2.6	1.4	146
Girls									
Grade 7	2.5	1.6	184	2.4	1.5	124	2.4	1.4	147
8	2.7	1.9	179	2.3	1.4	88	2.3	1.3	136
9	2.7	1.7	139	2.4	1.5	80	2.3	1.3	142
10	2.2	1.5	180	2.5	1.7	82	2.2	1.2	133
11	2.2	1.5	168	2.5	1.3	59	2.2	1.1	152
12	2.1	1.2	126	1.8	1.1	58	2.0	1.0	110
Total *ns*			1819			968			1646

	Sex	Grade	S x G	Sex	Grade	S x G	Sex	Grade	S x G
F	72.76	5.80	1.92	21.71	2.51	1.06	46.08	3.16	1.16
df	1/1807	5/1807	1/1807	1/956	5/956	5/956	1/1634	5/1634	5/1634
p	<.001	<.001	—	<.001	—	—	<.001	<.01	—

	F	df	p
Schools	20.38	2/4406	<.001
Sexes	124.53	1/4406	<.001
Grades	6.72	5/4406	<.001
Sc x S	2.74	2/4406	—
Sc x G	1.46	10/4406	—
S x G	1.48	5/4406	—
Correction for mean		1	

Scale 3: Conscientiousness

		School A			School B			School C		
Boys		*m*	*SD*	*n*	*m*	*SD*	*n*	*m*	*SD*	*n*
Grade	7	4.6	1.6	149	4.8	1.5	112	5.1	1.3	130
	8	4.6	1.6	148	4.8	1.6	111	4.7	1.3	127
	9	4.3	1.6	165	4.3	1.3	76	4.6	1.5	135
	10	4.2	1.6	160	4.0	1.4	57	4.5	1.3	138
	11	3.9	1.7	117	4.1	1.6	57	4.4	1.4	150
	12	4.0	1.4	104	4.0	1.6	64	4.4	1.3	146
Girls										
Grade	7	5.2	1.6	184	4.9	1.5	124	5.2	1.3	147
	8	4.9	1.8	179	4.6	1.4	88	5.0	1.4	136
	9	4.8	1.2	139	4.8	1.2	80	5.0	1.2	142
	10	4.9	1.5	180	4.7	1.5	82	5.0	1.2	133
	11	4.8	1.5	168	4.0	1.4	59	4.7	1.3	152
	12	4.8	1.6	126	4.8	1.4	58	4.8	1.4	110
Total *n*s				1819			968			1646

	Sex	*Grade*	*S x G*	*Sex*	*Grade*	*S x G*	*Sex*	*Grade*	*S x G*
F	65.53	4.84	1.32	14.65	4.94	1.92	22.74	7.06	1.0
df	1/1807	5/1807	5/1807	1/956	5/956	5/956	1/1634	5/1634	5/1634
p	<.001	<.001	—	<.001	<.001	—	<.001	<.001	—

	F	*df*	*p*
Schools	17.41	2/4406	<.001
Sexes	87.78	1/4406	<.001
Grades	15.17	5/4406	<.001
Sc x S	4.71	2/4406	<.01
Sc x G	<1.0	10/4406	—
S x G	2.12	5/4406	—
Correction for mean		1	

Scale 4: Anxiety and Guilt about School

	School A			School B			School C		
Boys	*m*	*SD*	*n*	*m*	*SD*	*n*	*m*	*SD*	*n*
Grade 7	4.7	1.9	149	4.8	1.8	112	4.6	1.7	130
8	4.5	1.9	148	4.3	1.8	111	4.3	1.6	127
9	4.5	1.8	165	4.4	1.6	76	4.2	1.7	135
10	4.0	1.8	160	3.8	1.6	57	4.1	1.5	138
11	3.8	2.0	117	3.6	1.6	57	3.7	1.4	150
12	3.5	1.6	104	3.6	1.6	64	3.6	1.6	146
Girls									
Grade 7	5.1	1.8	184	5.2	1.6	124	4.8	1.6	147
8	5.2	1.8	179	5.2	1.6	88	4.9	1.7	136
9	5.0	1.8	139	4.6	1.7	80	4.8	1.7	142
10	4.5	1.8	180	4.5	2.0	82	4.5	1.5	133
11	4.4	1.8	168	3.4	1.7	59	4.4	1.6	152
12	4.5	1.9	126	4.1	1.7	58	3.9	1.6	110
Total *n*s			1819			968			1646

	Sex	*Grade*	*S x G*	*Sex*	*Grade*	*S x G*	*Sex*	*Grade*	*S x G*
F	48.30	13.91	<1.0	15.43	16.01	2.03	37.44	13.30	1.02
df	1/1807	5/1807	5/1807	1/956	5/956	5/956	1/1634	5/1634	5/1634
p	<.001	<.001	—	<.001	<.001	—	<.001	<.001	—

	F	*df*	*p*
Schools	4.75	2/4406	<.01
Sexes	93.46	1/4406	<.001
Grades	39.88	5/4406	<.001
Sc x S	<1.0	2/4406	—
Sc x G	1.53	10/4406	—
S x G	1.27	5/4406	—
Correction for mean		1	

Scale 5: Favorable Attitude toward Teachers

		School A			School B			School C		
Boys		*m*	*SD*	*n*	*m*	*SD*	*n*	*m*	*SD*	*n*
Grade	7	4.6	1.6	149	4.6	1.6	112	4.5	1.5	130
	8	4.5	1.7	148	4.6	1.7	111	4.2	1.4	127
	9	4.5	1.7	165	4.8	1.5	76	4.4	1.4	135
	10	4.8	1.5	160	4.8	1.4	57	4.6	1.2	138
	11	4.6	1.4	117	5.0	1.5	57	4.6	1.3	150
	12	4.7	1.3	104	4.9	1.4	64	4.6	1.1	146
Girls										
Grade	7	5.1	1.7	184	5.4	1.5	124	4.9	1.5	147
	8	4.9	1.9	179	5.0	1.5	88	4.6	1.5	136
	9	5.0	1.6	139	5.1	1.6	80	4.4	1.4	142
	10	5.1	1.4	180	5.3	1.6	82	4.6	1.3	133
	11	5.5	1.1	168	5.1	1.5	59	4.8	1.3	152
	12	5.3	1.4	126	5.6	1.3	58	4.9	1.1	110
Total *ns*				1819			968			1646

	Sex	*Grade*	*S x G*	*Sex*	*Grade*	*S x G*	*Sex*	*Grade*	*S x G*
F	48.25	2.88	1.21	22.48	1.15	1.14	9.76	3.98	1.09
df	1/1807	5/1807	5/1807	1/956	5/956	5/956	1/1634	5/1634	5/1634
p	<.001	—	—	<.001	—	—	<.01	<.01	—

	F	*df*	*p*
Schools	29.31	2/4406	<.001
Sexes	76.62	1/4406	<.001
Grades	5.94	5/4406	<.001
Sc x S	5.37	2/4406	<.01
Sc x G	<1.0	10/4406	—
S x G	1.21	5/4406	—
Correction for mean		1	

Scale 6: Social Distractibility

		School A			School B			School C	
Boys		*m*	*SD*	*n*	*m*	*SD*	*n*	*m*	*SD*	*n*
Grade	7	4.7	1.9	149	4.3	1.7	112	3.9	1.7	130
	8	4.4	1.8	148	4.3	1.7	111	4.1	1.6	127
	9	4.7	1.6	165	4.5	1.4	76	3.8	1.4	135
	10	4.5	1.6	160	4.5	1.3	57	3.2	1.2	138
	11	4.4	1.6	117	4.6	1.6	57	3.5	1.3	150
	12	4.2	1.5	104	4.2	1.6	64	3.5	1.2	146
Girls										
Grade	7	4.5	1.9	184	4.4	1.6	124	4.2	1.6	147
	8	4.8	1.9	179	4.4	1.6	88	4.4	1.6	136
	9	4.7	1.7	139	4.0	1.4	80	4.3	1.5	142
	10	4.7	1.6	180	4.5	1.7	82	3.9	1.4	133
	11	4.5	1.6	168	3.9	1.5	59	3.7	1.5	152
	12	4.5	1.6	126	3.7	1.5	58	3.2	1.2	110
Total *n*s			1819			968			1646	

	Sex	*Grade*	*S x G*	*Sex*	*Grade*	*S x G*	*Sex*	*Grade*	*S x G*
F	5.38	1.33	<1.0	5.15	2.10	1.85	13.88	17.53	3.89
df	1/1807	5/1807	5/1807	1/956	5/956	5/956	1/1634	5/1634	5/1634
p	—	—	—	—	—	—	<.001	<.001	<.01

	F	df	p
Schools	87.29	2/4406	<.001
Sexes	2.36	1/4406	—
Grades	8.30	5/4406	<.001
Sc x S	7.12	2/4406	<.001
Sc x G	3.49	10/4406	<.001
S x G	2.78	5/4406	—
Correction for mean		1	

Scale 7: Orientation toward the Future

		School A			School B			School C	
Boys		*m*	*SD*	*n*	*m*	*SD*	*n*	*m*	*SD*	*n*
Grade	7	5.9	1.5	149	6.0	1.3	112	6.1	1.3	130
	8	5.9	1.3	148	5.9	1.6	111	5.9	1.5	127
	9	5.5	1.6	165	6.1	1.1	76	5.6	1.7	135
	10	5.7	1.4	160	5.9	1.3	57	5.8	1.3	138
	11	5.6	1.6	117	6.0	1.3	57	5.6	1.5	150
	12	6.0	1.0	104	5.8	1.5	64	5.7	1.2	146
Girls										
Grade	7	6.0	1.5	184	6.1	1.2	124	6.0	1.2	147
	8	5.9	1.6	179	6.3	1.1	88	6.1	1.2	136
	9	5.7	1.8	139	6.4	1.0	80	6.0	1.2	142
	10	6.0	1.4	180	6.1	1.5	82	6.0	1.1	133
	11	6.1	1.2	168	6.1	1.1	59	5.6	1.4	152
	12	6.1	1.1	126	6.3	1.2	58	5.8	1.2	110
Total *ns*				1819			968			1646

	Sex	*Grade*	*S x G*	*Sex*	*Grade*	*S x G*	*Sex*	*Grade*	*S x G*
F	9.24	3.53	1.54	9.96	<1.0	<1.0	4.11	3.58	1.07
df	1/1807	5/1807	5/1807	1/956	5/956	5/956	1/1634	5/1634	5/1634
p	$<.001$	$<.01$	—	$<.001$	—	—	—	$<.01$	—

	F	df	p
Schools	8.77	2/4406	$<.001$
Sexes	22.99	1/4406	$<.001$
Grades	1.67	5/4406	—
Sc x S	<1.0	2/4406	—
Sc x G	2.48	10/4406	$<.01$
S x G	<1.0	5/4406	—
Correction for mean		1	

Because there is a mass of detail to be recorded here, certain steps have been taken to simplify preparation of the tables. First, only negative correlations bear an algebraic sign; all others are positive correlations. Second, a single letter is used to identify the scales in the entries. The code is as follows:

L — Positive and Active Liking for School
D — Generalized Dislike of School
C — Conscientiousness
A — Anxiety and Guilt about School
T — Favorable Attitude toward Teachers
So — Social Distractibility
F — Orientation toward the Future

Note that the scale intercorrelations are given first for boys in the three schools, then for girls in the three schools.

Finally, refer to the footnote of each table for the number of students (n) in each of the sex groups in the table and the r necessary to be significant to reach $p=<.01$.

Intercorrelations of Scales for Boys, School A

	Grade	D	C	A	T	So	F
L	7	-.52	.63	.24	.61	-.28	.50
	8	-.35	.67	.20	.57	-.34	.25
	9	-.40	.70	.19	.42	-.47	.47
	10	-.39	.54	.16	.45	-.17	.50
	11	-.39	.65	.37	.42	-.28	.28
	12	-.25	.58	.17	.24	-.15	.41
D	7		-.48	-.01	-.49	.47	-.55
	8		-.48	.00	-.46	.49	-.37
	9		-.46	-.06	-.41	.51	-.45
	10		-.48	.06	-.38	.49	-.54
	11		-.47	.03	-.51	.54	-.41
	12		-.31	-.01	-.40	.46	-.36
C	7			.16	.59	-.30	.46
	8			.24	.48	-.30	.36
	9			.18	.53	-.42	.52
	10			.17	.43	-.31	.59
	11			.35	.55	-.40	.48
	12			.13	.43	-.30	.29

	Grade	D	C	A	T	So	F
	7				.18	.16	.18
	8				.06	.19	.14
A	9				.27	.10	.17
	10				.20	.08	.16
	11				.15	.03	.05
	12				.08	.06	.20
	7					−.36	.52
	8					−.31	.24
T	9					−.26	.45
	10					−.20	.50
	11					−.30	.43
	12					−.16	.42
	7						−.30
	8						−.31
So	9						−.43
	10						−.22
	11						−.23
	12						−.13

Grade	n	$p=<.01$		Grade	n	$p=<.01$
7	149	.21		10	160	.20
8	148	.21		11	117	.24
9	165	.20		12	104	.26

Intercorrelations of Scales for Boys, School B

	Grade	D	C	A	T	So	F
	7	−.34	.58	.18	.49	−.24	.41
	8	−.41	.68	.17	.58	−.41	.50
L	9	−.24	.48	.22	.27	−.18	.27
	10	−.48	.54	.19	.27	−.33	.20
	11	−.27	.23	.18	.40	.05	.30
	12	−.48	.61	.29	.23	−.35	.35
	7		−.48	.10	−.51	.58	−.64
	8		−.45	.00	−.38	.53	−.45
D	9		−.29	.06	−.42	.47	−.20
	10		−.36	.20	−.47	.57	−.48
	11		−.50	.07	−.37	.54	−.35
	12		−.41	−.20	−.29	.39	−.45
	7			.32	.56	−.29	.47
	8			.16	.51	−.52	.51
C	9			.31	.44	−.25	.28
	10			.33	.34	−.25	.35

	Grade	D	C	A	T	So	F
	11			.32	.43	-.43	.41
	12			.33	.26	-.41	.50
	7				.20	.19	.15
	8				.13	.05	.30
A	9				.24	.28	.19
	10				.06	.26	.01
	11				.20	.06	.20
	12				.13	.02	.30
	7					-.37	.45
	8					-.44	.46
T	9					-.16	.47
	10					-.23	.63
	11					-.26	.41
	12					-.14	.15
	7						-.41
	8						-.38
So	9						-.15
	10						-.08
	11						-.11
	12						-.34

Grade	n	p=<.01		Grade	n	p=<.01
7	112	.24		10	57	.34
8	111	.24		11	57	.34
9	76	.30		12	64	.32

Intercorrelations of Scales for Boys, School C

	Grade	D	C	A	T	So	F
	7	-.34	.51	.03	.46	-.19	.37
	8	-.55	.56	.10	.54	-.31	.48
L	9	-.49	.71	.16	.57	-.38	.54
	10	-.30	.38	.05	.27	-.15	.33
	11	-.38	.53	.07	.57	-.08	.54
	12	-.25	.44	-.01	.21	-.11	.20
	7		-.40	.28	-.50	.55	-.54
	8		-.54	.07	-.61	.63	-.56
D	9		-.58	.19	-.50	.63	-.56
	10		-.28	.12	-.45	.41	-.41
	11		-.46	.02	-.54	.34	-.53
	12		-.38	.16	-.40	.35	-.49

	Grade	D	C	A	T	So	F
C	7			.06	.43	-.37	.42
	8			.04	.47	-.45	.56
	9			.15	.45	-.43	.65
	10			.22	.26	-.14	.45
	11			.24	.56	-.17	.70
	12			.19	.23	-.23	.37
A	7				-.16	.28	-.07
	8				-.01	.14	.09
	9				.00	.21	.17
	10				.03	.09	.30
	11				.02	.19	.23
	12				-.14	.23	-.04
T	7					-.42	.37
	8					-.45	.49
	9					-.34	.55
	10					-.23	.35
	11					-.16	.64
	12					-.11	.34
So	7						-.37
	8						-.42
	9						-.36
	10						-.11
	11						-.21
	12						-.15

Grade	n	$p=<.01$		Grade	n	$p=<.01$
7	130	.23		10	138	.22
8	127	.23		11	150	.21
9	135	.22		12	146	.21

Intercorrelations of Scales for Girls, School A

	Grade	D	C	A	T	So	F
L	7	-.49	.61	.18	.46	-.35	.38
	8	-.54	.67	.24	.64	-.43	.53
	9	-.38	.67	.03	.53	-.43	.41
	10	-.37	.59	.20	.45	-.32	.46
	11	-.32	.55	.21	.37	-.38	.30
	12	-.29	.61	.07	.40	-.21	.22
D	7		-.55	-.12	-.55	.49	-.51
	8		-.58	-.10	-.57	.45	-.48
	9		-.58	-.01	-.47	.38	-.61
	10		-.53	-.05	-.49	.41	-.62

	Grade	D	C	A	T	So	F
	11		-.45	.09	-.41	-.46	-.41
	12		-.49	.01	-.42	.35	-.54
C	7			.30	.50	-.36	.41
	8			.25	.61	-.47	.49
	9			.11	.43	-.36	.49
	10			.25	.46	-.39	.49
	11			.12	.43	-.34	.50
	12			.14	.37	-.39	.49
A	7				.24	.07	.07
	8				.21	.03	.27
	9				.10	.15	.06
	10				.14	.01	.06
	11				.12	.13	.11
	12				.19	.09	.00
T	7					-.38	.40
	8					-.44	.49
	9					-.31	.39
	10					-.20	.55
	11					-.18	.34
	12					-.19	.38
So	7						-.26
	8						-.36
	9						-.35
	10						-.34
	11						-.23
	12						-.16

Grade	n	$p = <.01$	Grade	n	$p = <.01$
7	184	.19	10	180	.19
8	179	.19	11	168	.19
9	139	.22	12	126	.23

Intercorrelations of Scales for Girls, School B

	Grade	D	C	A	T	So	F
L	7	-.52	.52	-.08	.63	-.20	.50
	8	-.39	.50	.19	.44	-.26	.40
	9	-.37	.68	.15	.56	-.33	.49
	10	-.53	.57	.11	.12	-.16	.45
	11	-.29	.49	.16	.31	-.22	.33
	12	-.33	.51	.00	.59	-.48	.40

	Grade	D	C	A	T	So	F
D	7		-.48	.08	-.57	.41	-.62
	8		-.40	.09	-.44	.43	-.53
	9		-.44	.17	-.50	.52	-.40
	10		-.48	-.10	-.40	.31	-.50
	11		-.38	.11	-.46	.49	-.52
	12		-.40	.10	-.50	.44	-.56
C	7			-.11	.38	-.32	.40
	8			.18	.40	-.44	.37
	9			.16	.56	-.45	.52
	10			.33	.36	-.24	.55
	11			.24	.39	-.22	.36
	12			-.12	.48	-.36	.45
A	7				-.06	.12	.05
	8				.19	.10	.19
	9				.02	.04	-.11
	10				.13	.12	.22
	11				-.03	.00	.05
	12				.16	.12	-.03
T	7					-.21	.54
	8					-.26	.46
	9					-.47	.45
	10					-.17	.40
	11					-.11	.30
	12					-.40	.36
So	7						-.13
	8						-.30
	9						-.29
	10						-.04
	11						-.20
	12						-.22

Grade	n	$p = <.01$		Grade	n	$p = <.01$
7	124	.23		10	82	.29
8	88	.27		11	59	.33
9	80	.29		12	58	.33

Intercorrelations of Scales for Girls, School C

	Grade	D	C	A	T	So	F
L	7	-.46	.60	.02	.56	-.34	.54
	8	-.31	.46	.07	.50	-.19	.28
	9	-.29	.49	.03	.45	-.33	.31
	10	-.37	.49	-.05	.35	-.13	.32
	11	-.30	.51	-.08	.29	-.18	.38
	12	-.09	.44	.15	.25	-.05	.17

	Grade	D	C	A	T	So	F
D	7		-.45	.21	-.67	.56	-.58
	8		-.50	.10	-.48	.48	-.28
	9		-.50	.13	-.39	.41	-.53
	10		-.53	.09	-.32	.43	-.52
	11		-.39	-.01	-.41	.38	-.42
	12		-.32	-.01	-.16	.18	-.41
C	7			.03	.50	-.28	.47
	8			.09	.31	-.22	.34
	9			.18	.29	-.40	.49
	10			.13	.32	-.40	.47
	11			.25	.49	-.20	.54
	12			.22	.27	-.15	.37
A	7				-.02	.22	-.05
	8				-.02	.21	.04
	9				.00	.20	.02
	10				-.02	.15	.07
	11				.17	.22	.13
	12				-.01	.26	.10
T	7					-.40	.60
	8					-.24	.58
	9					-.27	.28
	10					-.22	.29
	11					-.18	.50
	12					.01	.22
So	7						-.33
	8						-.27
	9						-.35
	10						-.18
	11						-.18
	12						.05

Grade	n	$p = <.01$	Grade	n	$p = <.01$
7	147	.21	10	133	.23
8	136	.22	11	152	.21
9	142	.21	12	110	.24

Positive and active liking for school

5. If I have questions about something I have read outside class, I always try to bring them up in class.
8. I enjoy inventing or suggesting projects for work in school.
11. I think it's interesting to pull together all the different things I learn in one course or class.
20. I very much like to help the teacher with classroom chores, such as moving furniture, giving out papers, or cleaning the board.
30. If I see how to help a teacher plan or do something better, I am quick to suggest it.
40. I like very much to be with good students.
49. I very much enjoy learning new words.
60. If a classroom discussion gets confused, I feel I ought to help get things straightened out.
71. Some subjects interest me so much that I read a lot more about them than is required.
80. I like school and I like learning.
89. I get a lot out of classroom discussions.
95. I really like clubs or activities connected with school subjects that interest me.

Generalized dislike of school

6. If a lesson is difficult for me, I'd rather daydream than work at it.
15. I often wish someone would tell me why I have to go to school anyway.
48. The reason I learn is mostly to avoid trouble.
51. If I don't like an assignment or a discussion, I often groan to show how I feel.
66. I usually don't pay attention in class.
72. I always expect to be more confused after a discussion than I was before.
79. I often damage school property to show I don't like being there.
83. I hate school.
87. I just don't care whether a teacher likes my work or not.
90. I soon let teachers know they had better leave me alone.

Conscientiousness

10. If I know I am to be absent from school, I like to get my class assignments in advance.
14. I think students really ought to stick with something until they finish it.

25. To make sure I don't forget, I frequently go back over earlier lessons.
34. I like to read school books carefully.
46. I like to pay close attention to a teacher.
50. I try hard to make my written work neat and orderly.
54. I am careful to be prepared when I expect a class discussion.
61. I like to work hardest at my most difficult subjects.
69. I find that homework is almost always helpful in my learning.
76. I think it's important to plan my study time and my work.
81. I am very concerned about the quality of my schoolwork, and so I try to figure out my strong and weak points.
93. Before I hand in a test I check it carefully to make sure I haven't left anything out.

Anxiety and guilt about school

7. After I take a test I worry until I find out how well I did.
17. I think I could do better on tests if I could just stop worrying about them.
24. The thought of failure makes my hands perspire.
28. If for any reason I have to speak to the principal, I get nervous.
38. I worry a lot about school but don't like to talk about it.
43. I have had nightmares about not being able to do something correctly in school.
57. Sometimes when I don't understand something, I feel I really must be dumb.
68. Because I'm afraid I might not finish on time, I quite often work too fast and make mistakes.
77. If a teacher asks me to do something in front of a class, I am always afraid I am going to make some silly mistakes.
82. I worry about what my classmates think of me.
86. When a teacher says we are going to be given a test, my heart begins to beat faster.
94. If something happens to make me look foolish in school, I think about it for a long time afterwards.

Favorable attitude toward teachers

4. I like teachers who keep strict control of the classroom.
13. I think the best teachers are friendly but at the same time take no nonsense from the class.
*R 19. I think I'm just one more face to teachers most of the time: nobody special.
27. I feel that my teachers know a lot more about their subject than I do, so they can teach me a great deal.
R 32. I stay away from teachers because they're so bossy.

*"R" means that the scoring for the statement was reversed, as explained on p. 43.

35. I have been good friends with several of my teachers at one time or another, and I continue to like them.
R 53. It seems to me that many of my teachers are overly quick to be suspicious of a student.
R 64. It seems to me that most teachers care more about keeping order and quiet than about whether we learn.
R 67. Teachers put too much emphasis on learning facts and not enough on what they mean.
R 73. Most teachers are too old to understand the problems or interests of students.
78. I feel sympathetic with teachers because they have to do so much besides teaching.
92. I admire a teacher who can really take hold of a class and get it to learn.

Social distractibility

2. I think friendliness is more important than grades in being liked by other students.
21. If I am having trouble learning something, I'd rather ask a friend for help than go to the teacher or my parents.
31. I think there's no one you can depend on more than a close friend.
39. If I have to choose between spending time with a friend and getting something done for school, the friend always wins.
44. I welcome the chance to stop work at any time, if some other student wants to talk to me.
45. About the only reason I come to school is to see my friends.
58. I think having a lot of friends is important to enjoying school.
65. I have often stayed away from class just to do something with my friends.
70. I very often pass notes or talk to friends in class.
R 75. If anyone but the teacher tries to interrupt my work, I keep right on with it.
88. I like to have the same classes as my friends.
91. I care a lot more about having a good time with my friends in class than doing schoolwork.

Orientation toward the future

3. I think going to school is just about absolutely necessary for getting along in the world today.
12. I think the better educated you are, the better life you can lead in the future.
16. I am staying in school so I can get into college.
23. The people who quit school are some day going to be very sorry they did.
26. I want to go on learning the rest of my life.
33. I think the high school diploma is a necessary "ticket of admission" to many jobs and all colleges.

R 37. I'm pretty sure what's going to happen to me in the next ten years, and I don't think schooling has much to do with it.

52. I think that if you don't keep looking ahead to future life, you won't get the most out of school.

R 55. I think girls really don't need a lot of education because they will probably just get married and raise a family.

R 63. The world is changing so fast that most of what we learn now isn't going to be worth much in the future.

R 84. Most of what I learn in school isn't going to help in my future life.

R 96. I am going to quit school just as soon as I can, so I can get a job.

Favorable attitude toward the school as a social system

R 1. More freedom to make my own decisions in school would be very important to me.

R 18. Our principal treats us as though we're just things, not real people.

R 22. I think that except for a few requirements, the school should relax and let us learn what we want to learn, when we want to learn it.

36. I think the school has to have strict control of students in order to know who's doing what, where and when.

42. I feel schools *have* to have a lot of rules just to operate.

R 47. I think students are treated too much alike in school, even though we all know each is different from the others.

R 56. I like learning but I *don't* like school.

59. Even though someone else decides on them, I think the subjects we study here are the best ones for a good education.

R 74. I object strongly to having to have signed passes for every unusual thing we do.

85. Having a regular schedule of classes makes me feel secure about what's coming next.

Please do not write your name on this paper! (Some of you have done part of this before; please forget about your earlier answers.)

To begin with

There are lots of opinions about what our students think of schoolwork. Most of these opinions come from newspaper writers, parents, or other adults. People don't often seem to ask the students themselves what they think. This is what I want to do, and I ask for your cooperation in answering my questions.

As you will soon see, this is *not* a test, and there are *no* right or wrong answers. Instead, I shall ask for your opinions or attitudes on a good many things. You have noticed that I do not want to know your name. No one in this school will see your answers. This guarantees that you can put down exactly what you think. That's all that interests me.

What you are to do

In this paper there is a long list of statements of sentences that someone *might* say about school or schoolwork. Some of them are repeated in different words. You are to mark each sentence to show whether, *for you personally*, what it says is true, untrue, or something in between.

For example, a sentence might be "I think studying is a terrible waste of time."

	Very true						Very untrue
	7	6	5	4	3	2	1

Now, is that true or untrue for you personally? Notice that beside the sentence there is a row of numbers going from 7 at one end, which means "very true," through 4, which means "in between" or "don't know," to 1, which means "very untrue." *You are to circle the number that tells just how true or untrue the sentence is for you.* Many people, but perhaps not all, would feel that the sentence about studying being a waste of time is untrue for them. So I would probably find that many of you would circle a number somewhere on the "untrue" side, that is 3, 2, or 1.

158

Another example might be	Very					Very	
"Good work in school helps you	true					untrue	
later on."	7	6	5	4	3	2	1

Another example might be "Good work in school helps you later on." Many students would probably think that true. So most of you would circle 7, 6, or 5; but some would perhaps feel the opposite way and circle a smaller number.

How to do it

1. Circle one and only one number for each sentence. I cannot guess how many you will call true or untrue because that depends altogether on how you feel.

2. If you decide to change an answer, scratch it out so I will be sure to notice the change.

3. So many kinds of opinions are stated here that sooner or later you will need to use all the possible numbers to indicate how you feel.

Do not turn the page until we see whether anyone has any questions!

Circle the correct one

School_____   Grade_____   Male   Female   Your age_____

	Very true						Very untrue
1. More freedom to make my own decisions in school would be very important to me.	7	6	5	4	3	2	1
2. I think friendliness is more important than grades in being liked by other students.	7	6	5	4	3	2	1
3. I think going to school is just about absolutely necessary for getting along in the world today.	7	6	5	4	3	2	1
4. I like teachers who keep strict control of the classroom.	7	6	5	4	3	2	1
5. If I have questions about something I have read outside class, I always try to bring them up in class.	7	6	5	4	3	2	1
6. If a lesson is difficult for me, I'd rather daydream than work at it.	7	6	5	4	3	2	1
7. After I take a test I worry until I find out how well I did.	7	6	5	4	3	2	1
8. I enjoy inventing or suggesting projects for work in school.	7	6	5	4	3	2	1
9. Sports are more important than schoolwork.	7	6	5	4	3	2	1
10. If I know I am to be absent from school, I like to get my class assignments in advance.	7	6	5	4	3	2	1
11. I think it's interesting to pull together all the different things I learn in one course or class.	7	6	5	4	3	2	1
12. I think the better educated you are, the better life you can lead in the future.	7	6	5	4	3	2	1

	Very true						Very untrue
13. I think the best teachers are friendly but at the same time take no nonsense from the class.	7	6	5	4	3	2	1
14. I think students really ought to stick with something until they finish it.	7	6	5	4	3	2	1
15. I often wish someone would tell me why I have to go to school anyway.	7	6	5	4	3	2	1
16. I am staying in school so I can get into college.	7	6	5	4	3	2	1
17. I think I could do better on tests if I could just stop worrying about them.	7	6	5	4	3	2	1
18. Our principal treats us as though we're just things, not real people.	7	6	5	4	3	2	1
19. I think I'm just one more face to teachers most of the time: nobody special.	7	6	5	4	3	2	1
20. I very much like to help the teacher with classroom chores, such as moving furniture, giving out papers, or cleaning the board.	7	6	5	4	3	2	1
21. If I am having trouble learning something, I'd rather ask a friend for help than go to the teacher or my parents.	7	6	5	4	3	2	1
22. I think that except for a few requirements, the school should relax and let us learn what we want to learn, when we want to learn it.	7	6	5	4	3	2	1
23. The people who quit school are some day going to be very sorry they did.	7	6	5	4	3	2	1
24. The thought of failure makes my hands perspire	7	6	5	4	3	2	1

	Very true						Very untrue
25. To make sure I don't forget, I frequently go back over earlier lessons.	7	6	5	4	3	2	1
26. I want to go on learning the rest of my life.	7	6	5	4	3	2	1
27. I feel that my teachers know a lot more about their subject than I do, so they can teach me a great deal.	7	6	5	4	3	2	1
28. If for any reason I have to speak to the principal I get nervous.	7	6	5	4	3	2	1
29. I am pretty good at figuring out what answer a teacher wants without necessarily having learned anything to prepare for it.	7	6	5	4	3	2	1
30. If I see how to help a teacher plan or do something better, I am quick to suggest it.	7	6	5	4	3	2	1
31. I think there's no one you can depend on more than a close friend.	7	6	5	4	3	2	1
32. I stay away from teachers because they're so bossy.	7	6	5	4	3	2	1
33. I think the high school diploma is a necessary "ticket of admission" to many jobs and all colleges.	7	6	5	4	3	2	1
34. I like to read school books carefully.	7	6	5	4	3	2	1
35. I have been good friends with several of my teachers at one time or another, and I continue to like them.	7	6	5	4	3	2	1
36. I think the school has to have strict control of students in order to know who's doing what, where and when.	7	6	5	4	3	2	1

	Very true						Very untrue

37. I'm pretty sure what's going to happen to me in the next ten years, and I don't think schooling has much to do with it.
7 6 5 4 3 2 1

38. I worry a lot about school but don't like to talk about it.
7 6 5 4 3 2 1

39. If I have to choose between spending time with a friend and getting something done for school, the friend always wins.
7 6 5 4 3 2 1

40. I like very much to be with good students.
7 6 5 4 3 2 1

41. If I think assignments are too difficult, I complain to the teacher.
7 6 5 4 3 2 1

42. I feel schools *have* to have a lot of rules, just to operate.
7 6 5 4 3 2 1

43. I have had nightmares about not being able to do something correctly in school.
7 6 5 4 3 2 1

44. I welcome the chance to stop work at any time, if some other student wants to talk to me.
7 6 5 4 3 2 1

45. About the only reason I come to school is to see my friends.
7 6 5 4 3 2 1

46. I like to pay close attention to a teacher.
7 6 5 4 3 2 1

47. I think students are treated too much alike in school, even though we all know each is different from the others.
7 6 5 4 3 2 1

48. The reason I learn is mostly to avoid trouble.
7 6 5 4 3 2 1

49. I very much enjoy learning new words.
7 6 5 4 3 2 1

50. I try hard to make my written work neat and orderly.
7 6 5 4 3 2 1

	Very true						Very untrue
51. If I don't like an assignment or a discussion, I often groan to show how I feel.	7	6	5	4	3	2	1
52. I think that if you don't keep looking ahead to future life, you won't get the most out of school.	7	6	5	4	3	2	1
53. It seems to me that many of my teachers are overly quick to be suspicious of a student.	7	6	5	4	3	2	1
54. I am careful to be prepared when I expect a class discussion.	7	6	5	4	3	2	1
55. I think girls really don't need a lot of education because they will probably just get married and raise a family.	7	6	5	4	3	2	1
56. I like learning but I *don't* like school.	7	6	5	4	3	2	1
57. Sometimes when I don't understand something, I feel I really must be dumb.	7	6	5	4	3	2	1
58. I think having a lot of friends is important to enjoying school.	7	6	5	4	3	2	1
59. Even though someone else decides on them, I think the subjects we study here are the best ones for a good education.	7	6	5	4	3	2	1
60. If a classroom discussion gets confused, I feel I ought to help get things straightened out.	7	6	5	4	3	2	1
61. I like to work hardest at my most difficult subjects.	7	6	5	4	3	2	1
62. I feel comfortable and "at home" when I get into the school building.	7	6	5	4	3	2	1

	Very true						Very untrue

63. The world is changing so fast that most of what we learn now isn't going to be worth much in the future.

7 6 5 4 3 2 1

64. It seems to me that most teachers care more about keeping order and quiet than about whether we learn.

7 6 5 4 3 2 1

65. I have often stayed away from class just to do something with my friends.

7 6 5 4 3 2 1

66. I usually don't pay attention in class.

7 6 5 4 3 2 1

67. Teachers put too much emphasis on learning facts and not enough on what they mean.

7 6 5 4 3 2 1

68. Because I'm afraid I might not finish on time, I quite often work too fast and make mistakes.

7 6 5 4 3 2 1

69. I find that homework is almost always helpful in my learning.

7 6 5 4 3 2 1

70. I very often pass notes or talk to friends in class.

7 6 5 4 3 2 1

71. Some subjects interest me so much that I read a lot more about them than is required.

7 6 5 4 3 2 1

72. I always expect to be more confused after a discussion than I was before.

7 6 5 4 3 2 1

73. Most teachers are too old to understand the problems or interests of students.

7 6 5 4 3 2 1

74. I object strongly to having to have signed passes for every unusual thing we do.

7 6 5 4 3 2 1

75. If anyone but the teacher tries to interrupt my work, I keep right on with it.

7 6 5 4 3 2 1

	Very true					Very untrue	
76. I think it's important to plan my study time and my work.	7	6	5	4	3	2	1
77. If a teacher asks me to do something in front of a class, I am always afraid I am going to make some silly mistakes.	7	6	5	4	3	2	1
78. I feel sympathetic with teachers because they have to do so much besides teaching.	7	6	5	4	3	2	1
79. I often damage school property to show I don't like being there.	7	6	5	4	3	2	1
80. I like school and I like learning.	7	6	5	4	3	2	1
81. I am very concerned about the quality of my schoolwork, and I do try to figure out my strong and weak points.	7	6	5	4	3	2	1
82. I worry about what my classmates think of me.	7	6	5	4	3	2	1
83. I hate school.	7	6	5	4	3	2	1
84. Most of what I learn in school isn't going to help in my future life.	7	6	5	4	3	2	1
85. Having a regular schedule of classes makes me feel secure about what's coming next.	7	6	5	4	3	2	1
86. When a teacher says we are going to be given a test, my heart begins to beat faster.	7	6	5	4	3	2	1
87. I just don't care whether a teacher likes my work or not.	7	6	5	4	3	2	1
88. I like to have the same classes as my friends.	7	6	5	4	3	2	1
89. I get a lot out of classroom discussions.	7	6	5	4	3	2	1
90. I soon let teachers know they had better leave me alone.	7	6	5	4	3	2	1

	Very true						Very untrue
91. I care a lot more about having a good time with my friends in class than doing schoolwork.	7	6	5	4	3	2	1
92. I admire a teacher who can really take hold of a class and get it to learn.	7	6	5	4	3	2	1
93. Before I hand in a test I check it carefully to make sure I haven't left anything out.	7	6	5	4	3	2	1
94. If something happens to make me look foolish in school, I think about it for a long time afterwards.	7	6	5	4	3	2	1
95. I really like clubs or activities connected with school subjects that interest me.	7	6	5	4	3	2	1
96. I am going to quit school just as soon as I can, so I can get a job.	7	6	5	4	3	2	1

APPENDIX H:
Reliability Coefficients in School D

Grade	Positive and active liking	Generalized dislike	Conscientiousness	Anxiety-guilt	Liking for teachers	Social distractibility	Orientation toward future	School as a social system
Boys								
7	.69	.67	.79	.73	.46	.65	.42	.44
8	.73	.69	.74	.71	.59	.49	.59	.69
9	.71	.75	.77	.74	.57	.46	.54	.50
10	.71	.70	.77	.73	.62	.57	.59	.67
11	.72	.70	.76	.82	.48	.67	.13	.64
12	.70	.56	.72	.54	.49	.56	.43	.68
Girls								
7	.75	.69	.75	.68	.65	.52	.61	.67
8	.74	.75	.79	.65	.66	.70	.54	.59
9	.83	.81	.85	.76	.72	.63	.53	.64
10	.76	.72	.76	.68	.60	.67	.55	.63
11	.70	.73	.77	.67	.67	.61	.52	.74
12	.82	.74	.84	.74	.57	.74	.60	.60

APPENDIX I:
Analyses of Variance by Sex and Grade in School D

As in the across-schools comparisons in appendix D, the results presented here are based on a regression model. This again means that the highest order interaction was included in the residual. See appendix E for explanation of letter code used here.

	Grade	Boys m	SD	n	Girls m	SD	n		F	df	p
L	7	4.5	1.4	227	4.1	1.4	196				
	8	3.9	1.3	199	3.9	1.4	219				
	9	3.9	1.4	163	3.8	1.6	171	Sex	<1.0	1/2055	—
	10	3.6	1.3	162	3.7	1.3	151	Grade	12.15	5/2055	<.001
	11	3.6	1.4	125	3.7	1.3	151	S x G	2.17	5/2055	—
	12	3.9	1.3	130	4.0	1.4	149				
D	7	2.7	1.6	227	2.4	1.4	196				
	8	3.1	1.6	199	2.7	1.6	219				
	9	2.8	1.5	163	2.5	1.5	171	Sex	34.58	1/2055	<.001
	10	2.9	1.5	162	2.3	1.3	175	Grade	3.74	5/2055	<.01
	11	2.9	1.5	125	2.7	1.4	151	S x G	<1.0	5/2055	—
	12	2.7	1.3	130	2.2	1.2	149				
C	7	4.6	1.6	227	4.6	1.6	196				
	8	4.1	1.4	199	4.5	1.3	219				
	9	4.3	1.4	163	4.5	1.6	171	Sex	26.56	1/2055	<.001
	10	3.8	1.4	162	4.6	1.4	175	Grade	8.83	5/2055	<.001
	11	3.9	1.3	125	4.0	1.4	151	S x G	3.32	5/2055	<.01
	12	3.8	1.3	130	4.3	1.4	149				

	Grade	m	SD	n	m	SD	n		F	df	p
A	7	4.6	1.7	227	4.9	1.6	196	Sex	38.78	1/2205	<.001
	8	4.1	1.7	199	4.8	1.6	219	Grade	16.81	5/2205	<.001
	9	4.2	1.7	163	4.5	1.8	171	S x G	1.36	5/2205	—
	10	3.9	1.6	162	4.5	1.6	175				
	11	3.8	1.6	125	4.4	1.6	151				
	12	3.6	1.4	130	3.8	1.5	149				
T	7	4.3	1.4	227	4.5	1.5	196	Sex	15.06	1/2055	<.001
	8	4.1	1.4	199	4.4	1.4	219	Grade	6.41	5/2055	<.001
	9	4.6	1.4	163	4.7	1.5	171	S x G	1.14	5/2055	—
	10	4.2	1.4	162	4.7	1.3	175				
	11	4.4	1.2	125	4.5	1.2	151				
	12	4.6	1.1	130	4.9	1.2	149				
So	7	3.8	1.5	227	3.4	1.5	196	Sex	<1.0	1/2055	—
	8	4.3	1.4	199	4.3	1.5	219	Grade	10.01	5/2055	<.001
	9	4.1	1.4	163	4.5	1.5	171	S x G	5.01	5/2055	<.001
	10	4.3	1.3	162	4.6	1.4	175				
	11	4.3	1.5	125	4.5	1.4	151				
	12	4.4	1.3	130	3.7	1.4	149				
F	7	5.9	1.1	227	5.6	1.4	196	Sex	<1.0	1/2055	—
	8	5.6	1.3	199	5.7	1.3	219	Grade	1.58	5/2055	—
	9	5.6	1.2	163	5.7	1.2	171	S x G	2.89	5/2055	—
	10	5.5	1.4	162	5.7	1.3	175				
	11	5.5	1.1	125	5.5	1.1	151				
	12	5.5	1.4	130	5.6	1.2	149				

Grade	m	SD	n	m	SD	n
7	4.4	1.5	227	4.5	1.5	196
8	3.9	1.5	199	4.0	1.5	219
Sy 9	3.9	1.4	163	4.3	1.7	171
10	3.5	1.5	162	3.8	1.6	175
11	3.3	1.5	125	3.3	1.5	151
12	3.7	1.4	130	3.5	1.4	149
Total ns			1006			1061
N			2067			

	F	df	p
Sex	2.17	1/2055	—
Grade	23.98	5/2055	<.001
S x G	1.84	5/2055	—
Correction for mean		1	

See appendix E for explanation of letter code used here.

Intercorrelations of Scales for Boys

	Grade	D	C	A	T	So	F	Sy
L	7	-.32	.66	.30	.31	-.25	.36	.28
	8	-.39	.63	.27	.43	-.40	.36	.43
	9	-.39	.62	.41	.47	-.32	.35	.48
	10	-.49	.56	.23	.39	-.37	.34	.20
	11	-.19	.34	.10	.40	-.06	.29	.07
	12	-.27	.60	.09	.35	-.31	.13	.14
D	7		-.48	-.10	-.46	.63	-.40	-.56
	8		-.53	-.18	-.61	.47	-.45	-.58
	9		-.45	-.11	-.53	.49	-.48	-.60
	10		-.52	-.19	-.52	.52	-.49	-.46
	11		-.54	.10	-.57	.55	-.47	-.51
	12		-.41	.02	-.41	.32	-.46	-.35
C	7			.33	.34	-.41	.42	.33
	8			.41	.52	-.44	.38	.48
	9			.53	.45	-.45	.44	.42
	10			.35	.35	-.39	.33	.37
	11			.12	.35	-.40	.38	.36
	12			.25	.23	-.46	.17	.34
A	7				.06	-.03	.13	-.04
	8				.24	-.09	.29	.24
	9				.22	-.22	.26	.11
	10				.19	-.02	.20	.24
	11				-.10	.04	.13	.01
	12				-.10	-.02	.16	.22
T	7					-.39	.30	.49
	8					-.35	.39	.65
	9					-.46	.33	.62
	10					-.39	.37	.56
	11					-.23	.38	.50
	12					-.18	.41	.38

	Grade	D	C	A	T	So	F	Sy
So	7						-.32	-.47
	8						-.19	-.35
	9						-.19	-.38
	10						-.24	-.31
	11						-.14	-.22
	12						.02	-.21
F	7							.43
	8							.46
	9							.33
	10							.28
	11							.30
	12							.30

Grade	n	p = <.01	Grade	n	p = <.01
7	227	.17	10	162	.20
8	199	.18	11	125	.23
9	163	.20	12	130	.23

Intercorrelations of Scales for Girls

	Grade	D	C	A	T	So	F	Sy
L	7	-.48	.72	.27	.41	-.36	.51	.45
	8	-.41	.57	.20	.44	-.37	.30	.45
	9	-.54	.71	.26	.47	-.46	.46	.45
	10	-.35	.52	.09	.35	-.37	.36	.20
	11	-.42	.58	.13	.40	-.33	.42	.20
	12	-.27	.60	.09	.35	-.31	.13	.14
D	7		-.59	-.06	-.63	.60	-.56	-.64
	8		-.45	.04	-.56	.57	-.48	-.52
	9		-.60	-.26	-.66	.48	-.62	-.65
	10		-.44	-.05	-.59	.42	-.45	-.47
	11		-.53	-.32	-.52	.41	-.58	-.50
	12		-.41	.02	-.41	.32	-.46	-.35
C	7			.32	.48	-.47	.58	.55
	8			.40	.39	-.40	.39	.47
	9			.42	.53	-.58	.53	.54
	10			.36	.48	-.47	.47	.47
	11			.36	.43	-.34	.42	.39
	12			.25	.23	-.46	.17	.34

	Grade	D	C	A	T	So	F	Sy
A	7				.15	.05	.18	.19
	8				-.01	.10	.03	.09
	9				.21	-.10	.33	.22
	10				.11	-.03	.18	.26
	11				.27	-.07	.24	.21
	12				-.10	-.01	.16	.22
T	7					-.44	.51	.62
	8					-.46	.46	.53
	9					-.39	.50	.61
	10					-.43	.46	.58
	11					-.28	.42	.57
	12					-.18	.41	.38
So	7						-.29	-.42
	8						-.28	-.35
	9						-.28	-.38
	10						-.22	-.29
	11						-.22	-.24
	12						.02	-.21
F	7							.59
	8							.36
	9							.59
	10							.50
	11							.36
	12							.30

Grade	n	$p = <.01$	Grade	n	$p = <.01$
7	196	.18	10	175	.19
8	219	.17	11	151	.21
9	171	.19	12	149	.25

BIBLIOGRAPHY

Allport, Gordon W. 1967. *Pattern and growth in personality.* New York: Holt, Rinehart, and Winston.

Applezweig, M. H.; Moeller, G.; and Burdick, H. 1956. Multi-motive prediction of academic success. *Psychol. Reports* 2:489-96.

Borton, Terry. 1970. *Reach, touch and teach.* New York: McGraw-Hill Book Co.

Bronfenbrenner, Urie. 1970. *Two worlds of childhood: U.S. and U.S.S.R.* New York: Russell Sage Foundation.

Brownell, Samuel M., ed. 1971. *Issues in urban education.* New Haven: Yale University, Institute for Social and Policy Studies.

Clarizio, H. F.; Craig, R. C.; and Mehrens, W. A., eds. 1970. *Contemporary issues in educational psychology.* Boston: Allyn and Bacon, Inc.

Coleman, James S. 1965. *Adolescents and the schools.* New York: Basic Books, Inc.

———. 1961. *The adolescent society.* New York: The Free Press of Glencoe, a division of Crowell-Collier Publishing Co.

———. 1968. The concept of equality of educational opportunity. *Harvard Educ. Rev.* 38:7-22.

——— et al. 1966. *Equality of educational opportunity.* vol. 1. Washington: U.S. Government Printing Office.

Cottle, Thomas J. 1971. *Time's children.* Boston: Little, Brown & Co.

Donaghy, Rolla T. 1970. Factors associated with adolescent attitudes toward school and learning. *Diss. Abstr. Internat'l.* 31:1070-71.

Douvan, Elizabeth and Adelson, Joseph. 1966. *The adolescent experience.* New York: John Wiley and Sons.

Erikson, Erik. 1968. *Identity: youth and crisis.* New York: W. W. Norton and Co., Inc.

———, ed. 1963. *Youth: change and challenge.* New York: Basic Books, Inc.

Fantini, Mario and Young, Milton A. 1970. *Designing education for tomorrow's cities.* New York: Holt, Rinehart, and Winston.

Flanders, Ned A. 1970. *Analyzing teacher behavior.* Reading, Mass.: Addison-Wesley Publishing Co.

Friedenberg, Edgar Z. 1963. *Coming of age in America.* New York: Vintage Books.

———. 1959. *The vanishing adolescent.* New York: Dell Publishing Co.

Goodman, Paul. 1962. *Compulsory mis-education.* New York: Vintage Books.

Grambs, Jean D. 1965. *Schools, scholars and society.* New York: Prentice-Hall, Inc.

Gross, Ronald and Gross, Beatrice. 1969. *Radical school reform.* New York: Simon and Schuster.

Gross, Ronald and Osterman, Paul, eds. 1971. *High school.* New York: Simon and Schuster.

Group for the Advancement of Psychiatry. 1968. *Normal adolescence.* New York: Charles Scribner's Sons.

Heath, Douglas. 1967. *Humanizing schools.* New York: Hayden Book Co., Inc.

Holt, John. 1964. *How children fail.* New York: Pitman Publishing Corp.

———. 1969. *The underachieving school.* New York: Pitman Publishing Corp.

Jackson, Philip W. 1968. *Life in classrooms.* New York: Holt, Rinehart, and Winston.

Keniston, Kenneth. 1968. *Young radicals.* New York: Harcourt, Brace and World, Inc.

Matell, Michael and Jacoby, Jacola. 1971. *Educ. and Psychol. Meas.*, 31 : 657-74.

Melby, Ernest O. 1966. It's time for schools to abolish the marking system. *Nation's Schools* 77 : 104.

Nordstrom, Carl; Friedenberg, Edgar Z.; and Gold, Hilary A. 1967. *Society's children: a study of ressentiment in the secondary school.* New York: Random House.

Sarason, Seymour B. 1971. *The culture of the school and the problem of change.* Boston: Allyn and Bacon, Inc.

Sarason, Seymour B. et al. 1960. *Anxiety in elementary school children.* New York: John Wiley & Sons.

Silberman, Charles E. 1970. *Crisis in the classroom.* New York: Random House.

Tanner, J. M. 1962. *Growth at adolescence.* (2nd ed.) Oxford: Blackwell Scientific Publications.

Thelen, Herbert. 1967. *Classroom grouping for teachability.* New York: John Wiley & Sons.

———. 1970. Secularizing the classroom's semi-sacred culture. *School Rev.* 79 : 1-18.

Weinstein, Gerald and Fantini, Mario. 1970. *Toward Humanistic education: a curriculum of affect.* New York: Praeger Publishers.

Westinghouse Learning Corporation-Ohio University. 1969. *The impact of Head Start.* Office of Economic Opportunity.

Achievement-orientation, 86
Adelson, Joseph, 25, 33
Adolescents: chronological age, 5; parent relations with, 10-11; peer groups, 4, 25-27; problems of, 3-6; quality of adolescence, 5-6; questioning and doubting, 4-5, 14-16; reactions to investigations, 33-34; in school, 12-18; sex roles, 3-4; study of, 7-11
Analyses of variance: School D, 169-71; Schools A, B, C, 57-86, 140-46
Anxiety and guilt, 24-25, 44, 68-72, 84, 98, 120, 143; reliability coefficients, 49, 139, 168; School D, 102, 107-08; Schools A, B, C compared, 68-72; statement-scale correlations, 44 —intercorrelations with other scales, 97, 122; boys, 89, 91, 92; girls, 94-96; School D, 114-16
Applezweig, M. H., 75
Athletics, 26
Attitudes: in adolescence, 3, 41, 98; analyses of variance, 57-86, 140-46, 169-71; change of, 30; intensities and directions, 57-86; patterning, 87-97, 114-17, 121-22. See also School, attitudes toward
Autonomy, 14, 21-24

Boys: intercorrelations, 89-94, 147-50, 172-73; School D, 103-04, 172-73. See also Sex differences in attitudes
Bronfenbrenner, Urie, 26-27

Change in education, 19-30; evaluation of, 27-28; obstacles to, 28-30
Coleman, James S., 10, 19, 26, 27, 33, 61

Community: school and adolescent in, 17-18, 23; School D, 102; Schools A, B, C, 51-56
Competitiveness, 26-27
Conscientiousness, 65-68, 83, 98, 119-20, 142; reliability coefficients, 49, 139, 168; School D, 102, 107; Schools A, B, C compared, 65-68; social distractibility and, 85-86; statement-scale correlations, 44 —intercorrelations with other scales, 96, 122; boys, 89, 91; girls, 94-96; School D, 114-15
Cottle, Thomas J., 5, 29
Curriculum, 12-13

Data analysis, 43-49; correlations, 43-44; median (middle rating), 46-47. See also Intercorrelations; Reliability coefficients
Data collection, 48, 50-52, 103-04
Dewey, John, 16, 98-99
Dislike, generalized, of school, 62-65, 82-83, 98, 99, 119, 141; reliability coefficients, 49, 139, 168; School D, 102; Schools A, B, C compared, 62-65; statement-scale correlations, 44 —intercorrelations with other scales, 96-97, 122; boys, 89-91; girls, 94-96; School D, 114-15
Donaghy, Rolla T., 119
Douvan, Elizabeth, 25, 33

Erikson, Erik, 3, 33, 79
Evaluation, grading and, 23-24

Factor analysis, 38-40
Favorable attitude toward school as social system (School D), 102, 111-15, 121, 168
Favorable attitude toward teachers, 44, 72-75, 120, 144; reliability coefficients, 49, 139, 168; School D, 102, 109; Schools A, B, C com-

pared, 72-75; statement-scale
correlations, 44
—intercorrelations with other
scales, 96, 122; boys, 89, 92;
girls, 94-96; School D, 114-15
Flanders, Ned A., 15
Friedenberg, Edgar Z., 5, 8, 33,
60

General Anxiety Scale, 70
Generalized dislike. *See* Dislike,
generalized, of school
Girls: intercorrelations, 94-97,
150-52, 173-74; School D, 103-
04, 173-74. *See also* Sex differences in attitudes
Goodman, Paul, 5, 26
Grade levels compared: anxiety
and guilt, 70-72, 108; attitudes,
83-87; conscientiousness, 65,
67-68, 107; dislike, generalized,
of school, 64, 106; favorable
attitude toward school as social
system (School D), 112; favorable attitude toward teachers,
74-75, 107; intercorrelations,
93, 97, 116, 117; liking, positive
and active, for school, 61, 106;
orientation toward future, 79,
81-82, 110-11; social distractibility, 76, 78, 109; summary,
119-21
Grades: competition for, 26-27;
student attitudes toward, 23-24
Grambs, Jean D., 17, 19, 29
Gross, Beatrice, 28
Gross, Ronald, 10, 28
Group for the Advancement of
Psychiatry, *Normal Adolescence*,
3, 4
Grouping of students, 19-20, 58
Guilt. *See* Anxiety and guilt

Heath, Douglas, 19
History, 12-13
Holt, John, 23, 24

Identity, search for, 3, 12-13, 19,
21
Independence, 14, 21-24
Indifference point, 42-43
Individuality, 19, 21

Individuation, 93-94
Interaction term (S x G), 58
Intercorrelations, 38-39, 87-97, 121-
22, 147-53; boys, 89-94, 147-50,
172-73; girls, 94-97, 150-52, 173-
74; School D, 114-17, 122, 172-74;
Schools A, B, C, 87-97, 147-53
Interviews, 7-8, 33

Jackson, Philip W., 19
Jacoby, Jacola, 39

Keniston, Kenneth, 5, 8, 33, 60, 79

Level of significance, 43, 67-68
Liking, positive and active, for school,
58-62, 82-83, 98, 119, 140-41;
reliability coefficients, 49, 139,
168; School D, 102, 105-06;
Schools A, B, C compared, 58-62;
statement-scale correlations, 43
—intercorrelations with other scales,
96, 122; boys, 89, 91; girls, 94-96;
School D, 114-15
Liking for teachers. *See* Favorable
attitude toward teachers

Matell, Michael, 39
Melby, Ernest O., 26
Method: choice of, 33-40; use of,
41-56

National Merit Finalists, 55, 67
Nordstrom, Carl, 8
Null hypothesis, 57

Orientation toward future, 44, 79-
82, 86, 121, 146; reliability coefficients, 49, 139, 168; School
D, 102, 110-11; Schools A, B, C
compared, 79-82; statement-scale
correlation, 44
—intercorrelations with other scales,
96, 122; boys, 89, 92; girls, 94-96;
School D, 114-15
Osterman, Paul, 10

Parents: and change, 29; school and
community relations, 17-18; student relations with, 10-11
Patterning of attitudes, 87-97, 114-
17, 121-22. *See also* Intercorrelations

Peer groups, 4; cooperation in, 25-27

Personality structure, 87

Positive and active liking. *See* Liking, positive and active, for school

Psychoanalysis, 33

Psychological tests, 33

Questionnaires, 7-8, 33-36, 48; clerical problems, 50-51; composition of, 42-44; method of use, 34-38; privacy of, 134-35; School D, 100-04; School D, text, 158-67; Schools A, B, C, text, 125-34; student misuse of, 50-51

Reliability coefficients, 49-50; School D, 102, 168; Schools A, B, C, 48, 49, 139

Response set, 62, 64, 83

Restriction of range, 39

rs (intercorrelations), 88, 90

Sampling, 33-34

Sarason, Seymour B., 7, 28, 68, 70, 71, 84

Scales: composition of, 42-44; eighth scale added (School D), 100-01; reliability of, 47-48, 101-02; School D, text, 154-57; Schools A, B, C, text, 135-38; seven-step, 39, 42, 45-46; statement-scale correlations, 43-44; 12-item, 100. *See also* Reliability coefficients

Scholastic Aptitude Tests, 53-55, 103

School (schools), 7-18; administrators, 22, 29; autonomy of students, 14, 21-24; changes in, 19-30; community and, 17-18, 23; criticism of, 7, 10, 14, 16-18; curriculum, suggestions on, 12-13; quality of, 10, 52; radical students, 10; rules and discipline, 14, 22-23; students in administration, 23; tracking system, 19-21; ungraded, 21

School, attitudes toward, 8-11, 16-18, 98-99; patterning of, 87-97, 114-17, 121-22; as social system (School D), 102, 111-15, 121, 168; summary and comment, 118-23. *See also* Anxiety and guilt; Conscientiousness; Dislike, generalized; Favorable attitude toward teachers; Liking, positive and active; Orientation toward future; Social distractibility

School A, 41, 45, 102; description of, 53, 55-56; statement-scale correlations, 43-44

School B, 41, 44, 45, 102, 103, 116, 117; description of, 53-54, 56

School C, 41, 44, 45, 102, 103; description of, 64-65

School D, 41, 98-117; analyses of variance, 169-71; anxiety and guilt, 102, 107-08; attitude scales, 100-01; attitude scales, text, 154-57; conscientiousness, 102, 107; description of, 102-04; dislike, generalized, of school, 102, 106; favorable attitude toward school as social system, 102, 111-14, 121, 168; favorable attitude toward teachers, 102, 109; intercorrelations, 114-17, 122, 172-74; liking, positive and active, for school, 102, 105-06; orientation toward future, 102, 110-11; purpose of study, 99-100; questionnaire, 100-04, 158-67; reliability coefficients, 102, 168; social distractibility, 102, 109-10; summary, 120-22

Schools A, B, C: analyses of variance, 57-86, 140-46; attitude scales, text, 135-38; community relationships, 51-56; comparative analysis of, 57-86; intercorrelations, 87-97, 121-22, 147-53; reliability coefficients, 49, 139; statement-scale correlations, 43-44; summary, 118-23

Selfhood, sense of, 3, 12

Sex differences in attitudes, 9-10; anxiety and guilt, 70-72, 107-08; attitudes compared, 83-85; conscientiousness, 65, 67-68, 107; dislike, generalized, of school, 62, 64, 106; favorable attitude toward school as social system (School D), 112-13; favorable attitude toward

teachers, 74-75, 109; liking,
positive and active, for school,
60-61, 105; orientation toward
future, 79, 81-82, 110-11;
social distractibility, 76, 78,
109; summary, 119-21
—intercorrelations with other
scales, 97, 147-53; boys, 89-94,
147-50; girls, 94-97, 150-52;
School D, 116-17
Sex education, 4
Sex roles, 3-4
Silberman, Charles E., 7, 21, 23,
114
Sizer, Theodore R., 28
Social distractibility, 25-27, 44,
75-78, 85-86, 98, 120-21, 145;
conscientiousness and, 85-86;
reliability coefficients, 49, 139,
168; School D, 102, 109-10;
Schools A, B, C compared,
75-78; statement-scale correlations, 44
—intercorrelations with other
scales, 96-97, 122; boys, 89,

92; girls, 94-96; School D, 114-
15
Social studies, 12-13
Spearman-Brown Prophecy
Formula, 48, 102

Teachers: administrators' evaluation of, 22; and change, 28-30;
classroom management, 22;
and grading, 23, 26; and grouping of students, 20; and human
relations, 29-30; liking for
(*see* Favorable attitude toward
teachers); questionnaires administered by, 34-35; student
relationships with, 15-16, 22;
suggestions on questionnaires,
36-37; training, 21, 29-30
Test Anxiety Scale for Children,
70
Thelen, Herbert, 19-20
Tracking system, 19-21

Westinghouse Learning Corporation-Ohio University Study, 28